YOUNG, AUTISTIC AND ADHD

of related interest

So, I'm Autistic
An Introduction to Autism for Young Adults and Late Teens
Sarah O'Brien
ISBN 978 1 83997 226 3
eISBN 978 1 83997 227 0

All Tangled Up in Autism and Chronic Illness
A Guide to Navigating Multiple Conditions
Charli Clement
ISBN 978 1 83997 524 0
eISBN 978 1 83997 525 7

The Autism-Friendly Cookbook
Lydia Wilkins
Illustrated by Emily of @21andsensory
ISBN 978 1 83997 082 5
eISBN 978 1 83997 083 2

ADHD an A-Z
Leanne Maskell
ISBN 978 1 83997 385 7
eISBN 978 1 83997 386 4

Young, Autistic and ADHD

Moving into adulthood when you're
multiply-neurodivergent

Sarah Boon

Jessica Kingsley Publishers
London and Philadelphia

First published in Great Britain in 2024 by Jessica Kingsley Publishers
An imprint of John Murray Press

1

Copyright © Sarah Boon 2024

The right of Sarah Boon to be identified as the Author of the Work has been
asserted by her in accordance with the Copyright, Designs and Patents Act 1988.

Front cover image source: Shutterstock®.

A CIP catalogue record for this title is available from the British Library
and the Library of Congress

ISBN 978 1 83997 673 5
eISBN 978 1 83997 674 2

Printed and bound in Great Britain by TJ Books Ltd.

Jessica Kingsley Publishers' policy is to use papers that are natural, renewable
and recyclable products and made from wood grown in sustainable forests.
The logging and manufacturing processes are expected to conform to the
environmental regulations of the country of origin.

Jessica Kingsley Publishers
Carmelite House
50 Victoria Embankment
London EC4Y 0DZ

www.jkp.com

John Murray Press
Part of Hodder & Stoughton Ltd
An Hachette Company

MIX
Paper from
responsible sources
FSC® C013056

For Michael,
my grandfather

Contents

Acknowledgements		9
Disclaimer		10
Preface		11
1:	Introducing autism and ADHD	**16**
2:	Executive function	**40**
3:	Adulthood and decision making	**75**
4:	Relationships and social interaction	**113**
5:	Emotional well-being and mental health	**156**
6:	Identity and acceptance	**189**
7:	Conclusion	**225**
Glossary		230
Bibliography		232

Acknowledgements

Firstly, I have to acknowledge the wonderful autistic ADHDers who I spoke with and interacted with while writing this book. Thank you Star, Erin, Mark and Pavan for your contributions and sharing your own personal journeys. I have no doubt that what you shared throughout the book will be insightful and help other autistic ADHDers with understanding themselves a little better while trying to navigate this chaotic neurotypical world.

Lynda Cooper, thank you for taking the time to listen and develop my ideas when I first came to you (years ago now!) saying I wanted to write this book. Your direction and advice helped turn a daydream of mine into a reality of being a published author.

Also thank you to all the friends and family along the way who have been there for me during the book writing process. Whether that was making me a cup of tea as I spent my weekends and evenings writing or just listening to me vent when I experienced writer's block – you all know who you are!

Finally, I have to acknowledge my fur baby Milo. Although a cute distraction at times during the writing of this book, you never failed to brighten my mood.

Disclaimer

This book seeks to explore the common experiences that young autistic ADHDers have navigating the world. The contents of this book come from the lived experiences of autistic ADHDers, including myself, and fellow autistic ADHDers who I have interacted with or interviewed for this book. The contents of the book do not speak for all autistic ADHDers but seek to be a reference point for young autistic ADHDers as they go through early adulthood and the frequent challenges that come along the way.

Identity first language has been used throughout this book as it is the preferred use of language by most community members. 'autistic ADHDer' has been selected to describe people who identify as both autistic and ADHD in the book as it's the term best understood by most community members at the time of writing. However, I am also aware of people increasingly referring to autistic ADHDers (or themselves) as AuDHD online, and that the experiences AuDHDers have will likely also be reflected within this book.

The views and opinions expressed in this book are my own or those of the people who have contributed their thoughts, and are not my employer's or those of any of the other organisations and people I work with.

Preface

When I first started interacting with the neurodivergent communities, I noticed many of us identified as autistic ADHDers. I saw many conversations about the differences between being an autistic ADHDer and being 'just' autistic or 'just' an ADHDer.

Beyond casual conversations, there was very little out there in books or written in one place about autistic ADHDers' experiences. It felt as if professionals assumed people could only fit into one neat box set out by the DSM (the textbook psychologists and psychiatrists use to diagnose autism and ADHD). However, if being neurodivergent (in more than one way) has taught me anything, it's that humanity can't be fitted into nice neat little boxes. Even among autistic ADHDers we have a diverse range of experiences and views, despite sharing some commonalities on a neurological level.

Of the few books I did find on this topic, they almost exclusively had ableist (discrimination based on a person's disability or neurodivergence) takes on being an autistic ADHDer, including lots of focus on finding cures. Nothing that would be of any practical use to me as a neurodivergent person, or any neurodivergent person for that matter. When the literature is filled with neurotypicals telling us we need curing for not thinking like them, it's scary and dehumanising.

Being an autistic ADHDer in our neurotypical society is challenging, but I don't believe it's a solely negative thing. I see it as more neutral. There are both positives and negatives for all of us. It's certainly not the case that our lives are over once we discover our neurodivergence. On balance, learning I was an autistic ADHDer during my mid-twenties was a positive thing, and in some ways was just the beginning of the life I was supposed to be living (rather than craving normality for myself). I hope this book will provide a neurodivergent friendly perspective on autism and ADHD, where we are seen as part of the natural diversity of human minds rather than as a problem to be fixed because we are not neurotypical.

From getting to know many other autistic ADHDers, and through my own experiences, it's clear that one time in life that is not well understood for us is young adulthood. As the world tends to see autism and ADHD as 'childhood conditions', there is very little out there about what happens when we walk out of the school gate for the last time. It's as if the world thinks we suddenly become neurotypical (spoiler alert: we don't). Personally, this time of my life had some incredible highs, which I used to disguise the struggles I experienced entering adulthood. Ultimately, I was trying to act neurotypical without realising it. Although I didn't have the language at the time to discuss what I was going through, I just knew I had to 'fake it till I made it' for me to hold down a job that could pay the bills. But instead of making it, faking it led to a massive autistic burnout at 23 and unemployment due to mental health issues, which ultimately led to discovering the full extent of my neurodivergence.

Whether we know we are an autistic ADHDer at the time or not, most of us seem to face barriers when we enter the adult world, as our society is not set up with neurodivergent adults in mind. It is essential to remember that a lot of the time it's not our fault. This is why I hope that neurotypicals are reading this too, so they can unlearn their ableism towards us.

From my experience of working with autistic ADHDers, forming friendships with autistic ADHDers and being an autistic ADHDer myself, there seem to be some common themes around the barriers we face and the challenges we experience during the first few years of adulthood. Throughout this book, I will explore these common themes and specifically what they can mean for young autistic ADHDers.

Once I have introduced the concept of being an autistic ADHDer in more depth, we'll take a deep dive into executive function. Although executive function can be something we experience difficulties with across our lifetimes, there can a massive jump between the executive function demands of being a teen in school to starting a career and living more independently. This chapter will explore how to ease the transition of the executive function challenges we may experience going into further education and work, and keeping on top of everything at home (all at the same time)! Then, following on from the executive functioning in adulthood, we'll take a further look into the concept of 'adulting' and how we can decide as individuals what options are right for our own adulthoods.

Although relationships and social interaction have always been a part of our lives, we've often had to learn the hard way how we should interact with our neurotypical peers. However, the school playground has a different rule book to office politics and how adults interact (although there are some strong parallels!). We will focus on how the pressure to be sociable in a neurotypical way negatively affects us and how we can build more authentic relationships with different people in our lives.

With many of us being misunderstood throughout our lives as autistic ADHDers, our next theme will explore the impact this has on our emotional well-being and mental health, and how this can present differently to neurotypical people who experience distress. Also, we will look at finding alternative ways to manage our well-being and explore what works for us, as a neurotypical approach can often do more harm than good for autistic ADHDers.

Finally, we will look at perhaps one of the most important themes: identity and acceptance. Understanding who we are as autistic ADHDers can be difficult, especially if we have already had a lifetime of criticism and negative feedback for not being 'neurotypical enough'. However, leaving our childhood and teen years behind us can often be an opportunity to discover our strengths and how we want to live the rest of our lives. Self-acceptance can be hard in a society that still has a limited and outdated view of autism and ADHD. We will then conclude with how this is something we can work towards and which neurotypicals reading can learn from too.

Depending on what you are looking for, and what you want for your future, some parts of this book will be more relevant to you than others, so feel free to dip in and out throughout the book to the parts that are most relevant. This book is not written as a novel where all the pages need to be read in chronological order (trust me, I have never been able to read a book cover to cover in chronological order due to my own neurodivergence, so there was no chance of this book being written in such a way!). I fully appreciate that if you are looking to find out more about social relationships in your personal life right now then you might skip the sections on education and work for now and read what's relevant to you.

1
Introducing autism and ADHD

When most people introduce autism and ADHD, they will give academic and textbook definitions that quite frankly very few understand or can actually relate too! Also many of the formal definitions are based on old-school views that our neurodivergence is a problem and try to define us by only listing a bunch of deficits; not helpful at all!

Being mindful people will be reading this book from different levels of understanding of autism and ADHD, I will introduce both neurotypes (neurotypes are the ways our brain processes and responds to information in our environment) separately before describing what autism and ADHD can look like together as part of a package deal! I will provide a non-medical view of both autism and ADHD as I personally find the medical views dehumanising, and offer a more respectful and realistic view of autism and ADHD (based on lived experience), in everyday language that most should be able to understand. Next we will start to take a look at what it is like being both autistic and an ADHDer and how this is not the same as being autistic or an ADHDer.

While introducing autism, ADHD and being an autistic ADHDer, you may find you relate to certain aspects described and not others. That's okay, as most autistic ADHDers won't experience every single aspect of each neurotype (more on this later). This chapter is by no means a diagnostic tool, but simply acts as a guide to introducing autism and ADHD, and what it is like to be both autistic and an ADHDer in daily life.

Autism

Autism is a neurotype where a person will primarily have differences with how they interact socially, how they process sensory experiences, and their preference for repetitiveness and certainty compared to neurotypical people. These can manifest in many different ways, but below are just some common examples of what autism can be like for autistic people daily.

SOCIAL INTERACTION

- A natural preference for communicating about your interests over small talk during social interactions (sometimes referred to as info-dumping).
- Having your facial expressions or body language misread by non-autistic people, including people who you may know well.
- Focusing more on what people say to gather meaning from a conversation rather than on others' facial expressions or body language.
- Finding it easier to interact with people on a one-to-one basis or in a small group, compared to larger groups.
- Feeling the need to plan and script your social interactions in advance.

- Feeling the need to 'perform' during social interactions with most people, often referred to as masking or camouflaging. (On a side note, apparently small talk comes naturally to the non-autistics? Something I find truly fascinating and cannot fully comprehend.)
- Feeling the need to put in more effort to understand non-autistic and neurotypical people during social interactions.
- Finding most social interactions tiring and exhausting rather than energising.
- Finding it easier to socialise with autistic and/or other neurodivergent people.

With social interaction and autism, some aspects of how we socialise are often viewed through a cultural lens too. One prime example is eye contact, as where I grew up, eye contact is considered an important social norm, and a 'lack of eye contact' is something that many people and professionals look for when identifying somebody as autistic. However, in other cultures, giving eye contact isn't a social norm and can be considered rude or disrespectful. So, using a 'lack of eye contact' as an indication for autism does not automatically translate into other cultures. Also, many autistics in cultures where eye contact is valued feel pressured to give eye contact as part of their masking to blend in socially. So although many autistics will naturally have different ways of expressing themselves through facial expressions and body language, sometimes it may not be obvious they are autistic on a surface level due to pressures to 'fit in', avoid stigma and its potential consequences.

SENSORY PROCESSING

Autism affects all the senses, and not just the five you were likely taught about in school. Along with sound, taste, touch, smell and sight, there are three others: interoception, which is recognising your internal signals; proprioception, which is recognising where your body is in relation to other objects; and vestibular, which is your balance and how you move about in space. Autistic people tend to be more hypersensitive (oversensitive) or hyposensitive (undersensitive) to sensory input than neurotypicals. Below are just some examples of the hypo and hypersensitivities autistic people experience.

- Examples of hypersensitivity:
  - Finding loud and sudden sounds painful, e.g. fireworks or a siren.
  - Being overwhelmed by certain smells such as perfume and tastes, leading to a strong preference for bland food.
  - Being sensitive to textures, meaning that you can only wear clothes made from certain materials and need to cut out clothing labels due to the itchiness.
  - Finding certain patterns or bold colours too painful to look at, or finding fluorescent lights too intense.
  - May feel car sick from regular car journeys.
  - Always feeling some internal signals such as hunger and thirst.
  - Finding it difficult to be in small and crowded spaces.

The autistic ADHDers I spoke with shared some of their experiences with hypersensitivity:

66 I could tell the difference between my parents' footsteps as they walked around the house, I could hear every word of a television on low volume in a bedroom down the hall, and my parents learnt quickly that I had to be isolated in a quiet

room to do schoolwork because I'd stop and give my full attention to every little sound. There was never any such thing as 'background noise' to me.

66 Yeah, I think the worst thing for me is that I have really bad misophonia (negative responses and feelings towards some sounds) and for me, I think sound is the biggest thing.

66 Crowded lounges at my college became exhausting as I tried to focus on hanging out with my friends, while my brain forced me to pay attention to every other conversation, video game and explosion of laughter happening at the same time.

- Examples of hyposensitivity:
  - The need to feel deep pressure, which may mean you like tight cuddles, weighted blankets or deep massage.
  - Seeking out strong smells and food, e.g. you may have the need to have a lot of flavour in your food.
  - There may be certain sounds or music that you need to listen to and seek out.
  - You may love bright and bold colours, which can influence home decoration and clothing choices.
  - Not recognising needs in relation to bodily functions, e.g. not experiencing thirst, hunger and/or a full bladder until the need is extreme.
  - Not registering pain (or experiencing it less intensely).
  - Feeling the need to jump, bounce and move a lot.
  - Seeking the sensation of being on a rollercoaster and not experiencing dizziness.

An important point to note is that most autistic people are more sensitive in some areas of sensory processing and less sensitive in others. The example I gave above when talking about balance fully applies to me: I love rollercoasters – but cannot tolerate going over a road hump in a car (even at a slow speed). So even within the same sense, there can be a variety of responses from autistic people. It's very rare indeed to find an autistic person who is only highly sensitive to sensory experience, or is undersensitive to everything. Most autistic people will have a combination of both.

REPETITION AND CERTAINTY

Often autistic people need to follow routines and require a level of certainty to help us go about our daily lives. Some examples of this are:

- Experiencing positive emotions such as joy or relaxation from engaging in your interests. You may also find you enjoy doing the same (or similar) activities multiple times over or focusing on your interests for long periods of time, which is sometimes known as 'hyperfixation'.
- Experiencing and/or expressing your internal thoughts through repetitive movements or speech, more commonly referred to as stimming. Some examples of stimming are hand flapping, jumping, rocking and repeating phrases (or making noises) that feel satisfying. As well as experiencing or expressing our emotions, many autistics use stimming as a form of self-regulation.
- Needing some certainty of what is going to happen (or is planned to happen) ahead of time.
- Wearing the same clothes and eating the same food daily (although this could be mainly due to sensory processing too).

- A preference or a need to focus on one activity at a time, rather than constantly task switching.
- Finding comfort from following your own routines.

When I am referring to 'repetition and certainty', many others (particularly professionals) will refer to these aspects of autism as 'can't cope with change' or 'insistence on routines'. However, these views of autism feel like surface-level judgements (well to me at least) and don't reflect the reality of what other autistics and I experience. Often there are valid reasons why we stim, or hyper-fixate on certain activities, or need to follow a certain routine, which people may not understand unless they know us reasonably well. It's not that autistic people are incapable of dealing with things like change, but being expected to manage change within neurotypical expectations does not often work for us or becomes too overwhelming, as we do not experience, perceive or respond to the world in the same ways as most.

To remove the barriers that prevent autistic people from thriving, there needs to be an appreciation that our autistic differences may mean we need to stim or follow a routine in our own way as a form of self-care while navigating life, rather than assuming it is just a case of us not coping. It's also worth remembering that we can often mask distress when our individual autistic preferences for repetition and certainty are not respected (which happens a lot in a neurotypical-centric world), so it may not be obvious for others to notice when an autistic person experiences distress. Autistic or not, people in general often appear 'inflexible' or as if they 'cannot cope with change' when experiencing distress, so I do question how much of what is labelled 'inflexible' and 'rigid routines' is simply how autistics try to ensure their needs are met.

ADHD

ADHD is a neurotype where people will primarily have differences in attention, hyperactivity and impulsivity. There are three types of ADHD: inattentive ADHD (previously ADD), hyperactive ADHD and combined ADHD (both inattentiveness and hyperactivity). I will break down these three types and what they are like for ADHDers in daily life (as I just did for autism) rather than focusing on medical descriptions.

I will admit up front that I do not like the term ADHD to describe the neurotype as it's based solely on a deficit view. However, I have not come across a more neutral term to describe ADHD, so I will still refer to it as ADHD throughout this book. I am aware that some ADHDers will not agree with my stance (and that's okay), but my view is that if we automatically label every form of neurodivergence as 'disordered' by default, this can perpetuate stigma, which is why I hope for a more neutral way we can discuss ADHD in the future while still recognising both the strengths and the challenges it can bring.

INATTENTIVE ADHD

Inattentive ADHD is the term used to describe ADHDers who primarily have differences with their attention. Some examples of what inattentive ADHDers experience include:

- Finding it easier to carry out short-term tasks compared to longer-term activities.
- Finding it easy to start tasks but more difficult to keep your attention over longer periods of time (especially for repetitive activities you have no interest in).

- Your attention does not work in a linear way (meaning not following steps in a certain order which is expected by most people).
- Daydreaming a lot of the time, and sometimes when you were planning to carry out a different activity.
- Frequently misplacing objects you had in your hand only a few minutes before, e.g. keys and phone.
- Finding that sensory stimuli and other distractions affect your ability to complete a task or concentrate, when most others can ignore these with relative ease.
- Feeling as if it takes more effort than it should to complete long and repetitive activities.
- Finding it easier to process instructions which are written down and/or visual than verbal instructions.
- Realising that calendars and reminders are sometimes not enough to help with your organisation.
- Expending a significant amount of effort to run errands and stay on top of things such as paying bills, going to appointments and replying to messages.
- Have bursts of hyper-focus when you can focus on one activity for a period of time, and other times where you cannot focus on anything at all.

From having conversations with ADHDers and from my own experience, I find these are some of the frequently shared experiences when it comes to inattentive ADHD. Although in my day-to-day life, I do find inattentiveness can affect me in other ways. For example, even if I am reading a book I am enjoying, I find I can't read it for long periods of time (even if I want to). I often can only read the book in short bursts, have to do another activity and then come back to it later. By coming back to it later, I mean when I next remember, which could even be days, or weeks! Naturally, inattentiveness will affect ADHDers in different ways depending on what their daily lives look like. In education, inattentiveness could affect your ability to stay on a single task in the classroom while struggling to keep track of multiple deadlines.

Whereas for inattentive ADHDers in the workplace, it could be that standard email and calendar options don't fully support you to keep track of work and meetings. So although inattentive ADHDers may experience similar things, the impact this has on their daily lives can be vastly different, depending on the current responsibilities they have. Even for myself, I find that my ADHD will present differently depending on what environment I am in (to be honest, the same goes for my autism as well).

HYPERACTIVE ADHD

Hyperactive ADHD is the term used to describe ADHDers who have a stronger need to move and/or are more active than most people. Some examples of what hyperactive ADHD can look like include:

- Feeling the need to stim and move. For example, going between sitting and standing, when the neurotypical expectation may be to only stand or sit (may be referred to as fidgeting by some people).
- Frequently changing body position to feel comfortable.
- Having a sudden urge to run or climb and feel as if your brain is in autopilot mode.
- Say everything you are thinking all at once rather than wait to say it at another time.
- Joining in conversations when others don't expect it.

- Sometimes finishing people's sentences before they have finished speaking.
- Experiencing frustration when waiting in long queues.
- Hyperactive thoughts – going between different thoughts and ideas in your mind at a fast pace.

Hyperactive ADHD is often thought to only be seen in children who run around all the time and cannot sit still at all. While that is true for some, hyperactivity can present in many different ways. Just a few days ago I was at the theatre and I was struggling to sit in one position that felt comfortable, so at least every few minutes I was adjusting my position throughout the performance. I could not sit still as per neurotypical expectations and this is often referred to as 'restlessness'. Until I learnt more about ADHD, I did not relate to the stereotypical view of hyperactive ADHD; for many it does not present overtly all the time. For example, I find my thought process can be hyperactive at times but there is no way that an outsider would notice unless I told them about it.

COMBINED ADHD

As the name suggests, combined ADHD is when people experience both the inattentive and hyperactive sides of ADHD. Some people may be combined ADHDers but may be more inattentive or hyperactive. In my case, I was considered combined ADHD, but it was noted that I experience more inattentiveness than hyperactivity. So if you relate to aspects of both inattentive and hyperactive ADHD, but find you fit one subtype more than another, then you still may be considered a combined ADHDer. Others may experience equal (or similar) levels of inattentiveness and hyperactivity with their combined ADHD.

Similar to autistic people, ADHDers have spoken about the need to mask their neurodivergence (at great emotional cost) to be safe and treated with respect by others. So it is vital to understand that somebody may not appear like they have ADHD through brief interactions, due to societal pressures to hide it (or they do not fit into the narrow demographic and stereotypical view of ADHD as the 'naughty white boy'). ADHD is something that is experienced internally, so although you may see indications through interacting with an ADHDer, you can never truly know if somebody is an ADHDer unless they disclose it to you, or if they describe their own experiences.

Autism and ADHD together

Now you are probably thinking after reading the description for ADHD that in some ways it conflicts with how I described autism, and in other ways ADHD overlaps with my description of autism. Those are both reasonable assumptions to make, as many autistic ADHDers describe how the lines can feel blurred as to what is their autism and what is their ADHD, or they describe their autism and ADHD as almost being interwoven with each other and impossible to fully disentangle, whereas others see their ADHD 'side' and autism 'side' constantly butting heads with each other! An autistic ADHDer interviewee I spoke with commented on this matter by describing their neurodivergence as:

> It's almost this weird thing of feeling like in a way sometimes the traits can cancel each other out. But then at the same time, it doesn't do that in a way that makes me feel neurotypical in any way, it's more of a kind of having like two sides of your personality that kind of pop out at different moments.

Personally, I lean more towards seeing my autism and ADHD as being interwoven with each other as I feel that my brain doesn't entirely fit into stereotypical understandings of either autism or ADHD. The best way to explain this is by giving some examples of my autistic ADHDer experience. One example is the stereotype that autistic people have excellent attention to detail, whereas ADHDers do not. However, I find that I will notice certain details and hyper-focus on them, to the point where I miss all the other details. So there are elements of both autism and ADHD at play when it comes to my attention to detail, but it manifests in a way that does not fit into standard definitions of either autism or ADHD. Some people I have talked with about being an autistic ADHDer have asked if they cancel each other out to make me 'normal'. I can guarantee you they do not! Otherwise I wouldn't have been identified as autistic or an ADHDer.

Another one of the autistic ADHDers who I chatted with shared how their autism and ADHD can contradict each other at times:

66 Whereas for me, I learnt why my autism was more like, okay, we've got to follow the rules. Like we can't just get up and go walk about, we can't just stare out the window. We've got to sit here and try. But then that's where fidget toys came in. I would pick up a pen and just sort of move it around and I just couldn't have something still in my hand. It's like, if I need to concentrate I need to fidget.

So although their autism meant they wanted to follow the rules, their ADHD meant that this could be very challenging. I certainly related to this, as during school I never wanted to be seen breaking the rules, but this clashed with my need to fidget to concentrate. It meant that over the years I became very savvy at learning to fidget in ways that wouldn't be seen by others (mainly finding a small object to fidget with under the desk!).

Also, a prime example of autistic ADHDers not fitting into traditional views of autism and ADHD is routine. Many autistic people need their routine to manage the day whereas ADHDers tend to have difficulties following routines. So what can this mean for autistic ADHDers?

I can only speak for myself: I do see the benefits of routines but I find them incredibly hard to follow. I have described it before as 'I need routine to get myself organised but I struggle to get myself organised enough to start to follow a routine'. So it feels a bit like a chicken or egg issue, it's hard to know what came first which triggered the never-ending cycle! I find that sometimes my frustration of wanting to follow a routine but being unable to means I just sit there and don't get anything done.

When autistic ADHDers describe their ADHD 'side' and autism 'side' constantly being in battle with each other, they often give an example of their experiences with routine and one of the autistic ADHDers I spoke with shared how they experience these two sides of their neurodivergence when it comes to following a schedule:

> I'm the sort of person who wants to have a schedule and then I don't want to have a schedule! I want the schedule as I crave certainty and structure. That is the autism side of me. But then the ADHD side of me wants to rip up that schedule and I just want something that is different, and have the excitement of doing things as they come, and not having to stick with boring schedules.

If I am being honest, routine is the one area where it does feel as if the autism and ADHD are fighting each other in my brain (metaphorically, not literally), which is why I end up struggling to do anything during these moments, even when I need and want to. I do not experience this constantly, but enough that it interferes with my daily life.

Similar to routine, many autistic ADHDers have an interesting relationship with change. Autistic people are viewed as hating change, while ADHDers are seen as seeking change all the time. I am a fan of change and sometimes I do feel the need for change. In the first few years of working full time, I didn't stay in a job for longer than a year, and this was in part due to my need for change. There were other reasons too, but I will talk about them in more depth in a later chapter. So although it may seem like my ADHD side is more prevalent when it comes to change, there are times where it definitely intersects with my autism. Like most autistic people, I have my interests which I enjoy deeply. However, my interests do change over time. Although there have been some consistent interests over the years (my interest in Disney and *The Sims* has been around for 20+ years), some of them can change frequently. For example, I was into doing crosswords a lot of the time for about a month or two. Then I suddenly got bored and needed a change in how I spent my free time. So I would say that my ADHD means that my autistic interests can come and go more frequently than autistics who are not ADHDers too.

So although ADHD and autism can conflict with each other in some ways, there are areas where they overlap as well! One example is executive functioning (which we will take a deeper look at in the next chapter), which primarily affects our planning, organisation and short-term memory. Also differences in sensory processing have been associated with ADHD, which is more commonly understood to be part of autism. The areas where autism and ADHD can overlap is why I believe it's almost impossible for autistic ADHDers (and professionals) to fully disentangle what is autism and what is ADHD for us.

Sensory processing is often a significant part of autistic people's daily lives. However, if we are ADHDers too, it can also impact how we process sensory information and our ability to choose which sensory input to focus on.

66 ADHD means my brain can't filter out or prioritise information, and I hear and see everything that's going on around me, all the time.

So although we may be hypersensitive to sensory input due to our autism, if we are in a busy environment, with multiple noises and lots of visual information, our ADHD can make it difficult to filter the information. The combination of being hypersensitive to sensory input, along with being unable to filter out all the different forms of sensory input we experience at once, may mean some autistic ADHDers could be more vulnerable to sensory overwhelm, leading to meltdowns or shutdowns, or it taking less sensory input for us to feel overwhelmed. One of the autistic ADHDers I spoke with shared how sensory overwhelm can lead to meltdowns:

66 Obviously it does affect my sensory experiences because of how I perceive the world differently and the way my head processes sensory experiences. I can get easily overstimulated and it is easy for me to experience meltdowns as a result of sensory hell!

On a personal level, I have experienced sensory overwhelm too, which has led to meltdowns and shutdowns. I think this is part of the reason why I love my noise cancelling headphones, as they do the job of filtering out all the noises my brain cannot, and I can choose to only hear one noise/sound or piece of music at a time, which is pleasing for my senses and can help to improve my focus.

Being an autistic ADHDer means that our experiences are not fully reflected within the labels of autism or ADHD on their own, but I should add that being an autistic ADHDer is not formally recognised as its own neurotype; they are considered separate neurotypes that can commonly co-exist together. However, who knows what the future may bring as our understanding of both autism and ADHD grows and develops over time.

Identification, self-diagnosis and formal diagnosis

66 I don't think my life would have been perfect if I was diagnosed (while growing up), but I think at least I would have understood myself a bit better in some ways.

To get a diagnosis or not to get a diagnosis? That is the question that causes a lot of debate among neurodivergent people. But before going in-depth on how to decide if going for a diagnosis is the right option for you (if you haven't received one yet), there are a few things to clarify.

Firstly, diagnosis is not compulsory; it is always your choice if you decide to go through the diagnostic process for autism and

ADHD. Nobody should ever pressure you to get a formal diagnosis and if they do then that is abusive. Remember, being an autistic ADHDer is not a life or death situation, so not having a diagnosis does not mean that you will be missing out on medical treatments that your body needs to survive. Also autism and ADHD are lifelong and a diagnosis doesn't change your neurodivergence, it just formally recognises it.

Secondly, self-diagnosis is always an option. If you are content with knowing you are an autistic ADHDer after doing your research into autism and ADHD, then self-identification is a choice you can make. Although some will gatekeep on people's diagnosis (or presumed diagnosis) status, only you know the full reality of your experiences. Many people face barriers in accessing a diagnosis, ranging from financial reasons to years-long waiting lists to the diagnostic criteria being based on a narrow demographic (white, cis-male children). Autistic ADHDers who fall outside that narrow demographic or who cannot afford autism and ADHD assessments (which is most of us) will likely face barriers when accessing a diagnosis, and it is for this reason why I see gatekeeping people for not having a formal diagnosis as a form of discrimination.

When interviewing fellow autistic ADHDers, some felt that when they were beginning to realise they were neurodivergent, their experiences did not align with more common and stereotypical views.

❝❝ A lot of these samples were like, young boys, basically. That was all it was. But then there were elements of that that I did relate to.

In an ideal world, autism and ADHD would not need to be 'diag-nosed', in a way which implies they are diseases that need curing to prevent death or permanent damage to our bodies, which is not the case with autism and ADHD. Personally I would like to see a less medical and more affirming way that people can recognise their autism and ADHD and access support if they need it (although people would still need to access a doctor if they wanted ADHD medication). However, that is not the reality at the time of writing, and sadly we still live in a society where diagnosis (a long and/or expensive process) is often the only way we can access support we need, so it is necessary to consider if we should be going for a diagnosis or not.

There is no clear-cut answer as to whether people should get a formal diagnosis or not; it is often entirely dependent on your personal situation whether it is in your best interest. There are pros and cons with both options but ultimately it's up to you if you decide to pursue a formal diagnosis. So I am not going to give a lecture about which option is better. However, what I will do is suggest questions you can ask yourself if you're debating getting a diagnosis, so you can figure out what the best option is for you. I did choose to get a formal diagnosis for both my autism and ADHD, but that doesn't mean you have to.

I do think having more than one form of neurodivergence can act as a barrier to receiving an accurate diagnosis. As autistic ADHDers tend not to fit neatly into the tick boxes for autism and ADHD, it means unless a diagnostician has a reasonable level of expertise in both autism and ADHD, they can be easily missed.

Also, many professionals' and diagnosticians' views of both au-tism and ADHD can be one-sided, as their training often comes

Pros	Cons
• Able to use your diagnosis to access support.	• It's a long, draining process.
• You have the paperwork if you ever need to officially disclose you are autistic.	• It can feel intrusive, depending on how much depth the assessment goes into.
• Better understanding of how your autism and ADHD affects you.	• Discussing potentially traumatic events from the past.
• Easier to advocate for accommodations and adjustments at work and in education.	• It is expensive and/or there's a long wait for an assessment.
• One form of validation and better understanding of self.	• Some people will question the validity of your diagnosis/ diagnoses because you are not like their best friend's 'autistic ADHDer nephew' (I wish I was joking with this one).
• May help the people in your life understand you better.	• Some countries discriminate against people with an autism diagnosis if they try to immigrate to other countries.
• Stronger legal protections against ableism you may face.	
• Access to ADHD medication.	• Some health services do discriminate based on a diagnosis.
• A reduction in labelling yourself as 'lazy', and can reduce self-loathing due to better understanding of yourself.	• People will make assumptions about you based on a diagnosis before getting to know you as a person.
• Can be part of a healing journey from past events.	• It can lead to new forms of stigma from people who are less understanding.
• Self-acceptance of non-neurotypical behaviours, e.g. stimming.	• There may be changes in dynamics with friends and in relationships based on their preconceptions of autism and ADHD.
• Feeling less pressure to 'mask' in some situations.	
	• Potentially new or additional forms of discrimination

from only a medical perspective, which makes assumptions about autism and ADHD from observing us from the outside, rather than how we experience autism and ADHD on a daily basis. As a consequence, it can be hard to relate to medical descriptions of our neurodivergence on a personal level, as one of the autistic ADHDers explained:

> ❝ I was diagnosed with ADHD very early, at seven years old. I've always related to most of the definitions and examples my parents presented to me in little self-help books. I never related to similar descriptions of children with autism, until I started exploring the online neurodivergent community as an adult.

So although some people may see themselves and/or their experiences represented in medical definitions of autism and ADHD, this may not necessarily inform us of the full picture of our own neurodivergence. We can also gain knowledge and understanding about our neurodivergence from interacting with other autistic ADHDers who share similar experiences to ourselves. For myself, receiving my diagnoses was just the starting point of learning about autism and ADHD; I felt I learnt a lot more over the years through interacting with other neurodivergent adults.

Also from speaking with others and from my own experience, receiving a diagnosis can affect us for a period of time afterwards. There can be relief from better understanding ourselves and a lot more things making sense, but also a lot of grief from past situations and anger at the ableism we have experienced over the years. It is something that often isn't talked about by the professionals carrying out the diagnosis, and to some extent I am not sure they are all aware of the emotional process of receiving a late diagnosis. It is something to consider when deciding to get a diagnosis if you didn't receive one as a child. Personally, I do not regret my decision to go for an autism and ADHD diagnosis, but I was not aware of the full emotional impact it would have afterwards and knowing that this is a common experience post diagnosis would have been helpful.

Monotropism – a new way of understanding autism and ADHD?

Monotropism is a theory by Dinah Murray and Wenn Lawson (Murray, 2022) that was initially created to describe how autistic people think (although some non-autistic people may also relate to monotropism), where a person's attention tends to focus on one or a small number of interests in more depth, creating an 'attention tunnel' which means they cannot (or struggle to) focus on anything outside their attention tunnel. The attention tunnel seeks to explain experiences that are common among autistic people. For example, disruptions from too much sensory input from outside our attention tunnel can lead to sensory overload. It also can explain why our interests are so valuable to us and how some can only focus on one aspect of social interaction at one time, meaning we can experience difficulties such as keeping track of the conversation in a large group and need more time to process information outside the attention tunnel. As within a conversation, there can often be several things happening at once. Also many autistic ADHDers can experience hyper-focus at times, and monotropism is one way that can describe why we can devote our whole attention to one activity for a period of time. For myself, it certainly explains how when I would start playing *The Sims* after school, because I was so focused on the game, any sense of time disappeared and it was 2 am before I knew it!

From my interactions with neurodivergent communities, some who previously considered themselves autistic ADHDers are now identifying as monotropic, as they feel monotropism better describes their experiences than how autism and ADHD are currently understood. As monotropism is not a medical term, people are not diagnosed as monotropic, but it is an experience neurodivergent people identify with. As an autistic ADHDer, you may find that monotropism also describes the way you experience your neurodivergence and perhaps more so than autism and ADHD do together. Monotropism as a theory is increasing in popularity and is being spoken about a lot more, so I would highly recommend looking into the concept further (Murray, 2022) to see if it helps you to understand how your attention may work and decide if monotropism makes sense for you and describes how your thinking process works.

As you continue reading this book, you may find that some of the concepts and examples mentioned could be related to or explained by monotropic thinking. So it is something to bear in mind that may help understand how you think a little better. Also if you are an autistic ADHDer who does not fully relate to the monotropism theory, that is okay as there is no one way of being an autistic ADHDer. We are all unique individuals, and the commonly used phrase 'When you've met one autistic person, you have met one autistic person' also applies to us autistic ADHDers!

Also, I have come across some autistic ADHDers relating to parts of monotropism, but not fully. One example is jumping between a few different areas of focus due to the impulsivity and attention differences in ADHD. However, anything that falls outside their select hyper-focuses (or attention tunnels) can be very difficult to transition to. I would say this is closer to my experience too at times, as I find it exhausting (or impossible) to be focused on one single thing for hours on end (with *The Sims* being one of the few exceptions!).

Now that we have introduced what autism and ADHD are, some of the commonly shared experiences of autistic ADHDers, and monotropism, it seems like the right time to explore some of the concepts that have been mentioned in this chapter in more depth, starting with executive functioning.

2
Executive function

Executive function is a term that is often used by professionals to describe how our brains process information and work to complete tasks often related to organising and planning. Often when we are trying to focus our attention, remember instructions and carry out multiple tasks in order to achieve a goal, our brains are relying on our executive function abilities. Differences in executive functioning certainly affect most (if not all) autistic ADHDers navigating the demands of daily life in a neurotypical world.

This chapter will look at the concept of executive functioning using everyday language, exploring the four main areas of executive functioning in which autistic ADHDers tend to experience differences from neurotypicals. These are: short-term memory, task switching (including the relatively recent concept of autistic inertia), impulsivity and sequencing, along with how these areas of executive function can lead to time blindness. We will then take a look at how executive functioning affects us in education, at work and home while also going through some strategies that can help make life that little bit easier.

Short-term memory

If you ever hear a professional say the term 'working memory' what they are usually referring to is what many people call 'short-term memory'. Short-term memory is the thinking process people use to hold certain thoughts in their mind for a short period of time. People will often use their short-term memory to complete a quick task, follow several instructions at once or find something they need to use immediately.

An example of when people use their short-term memory would be when you are ordering several coffees in a café and the server doesn't have a notepad to write down the order – they will need to use their short-term memory to remember the several items on the order. Some people can remember everything with ease, create several drinks and fulfil the order using their short-term memory. However, for us autistic ADHDers who may experience difficulties with our short-term memory, things are not exactly this straightforward. We may be able to remember up to two or three items on the order, but our brains may struggle with anything more or not be able to process it. To remember all the details, we would likely need to write it down, use technology on our phones or find an alternative way to note down the full order to see what is needed to fulfil it.

As well, some autistic ADHDers may rely on following written or visual instructions to complete a task successfully, especially if it involves a lot of steps. Some may find that they need these instructions every time they carry out the task, whereas others may only need it when they start something new for the first time, until it becomes a more automatic process.

Another prime example of our short-term memory would be reading a text message and thinking 'I am going to reply to that later', and then forgetting as my mind switches to doing something else, without remembering that I need to go back and reply to the text. I have lost count of the number of times I have done this! Particularly when it is a long message, or I am being asked something that I can't provide an answer to on the spot. Also if we forget where we left our keys all the time as they are not right in front of us, and are constantly looking everywhere to try and find them, then that is another prime example of the short-term memory differences we have.

Although some of us experience difficulties with short-term memory, this does not tend to have an impact on our long-term memory, as it is not the same process in the brain. One thing I have seen in other autistic ADHDers (and experience myself) is that some of us who struggle with short-term memory have average or even good long-term memories.

In my daily life, I often forget where I left my phone five minutes ago due to my short-term memory difficulties, but I have memories from a very young age. One example is I can clearly remember when Princess Diana died despite only being two years old at the time! Most people my age, in contrast, do not have in-depth memories from two years old. I do not have savant like abilities of any kind (despite the Rain Man stereotype of autism) but I do have several long-term memories I can remember in significant detail, to the point where it can freak out some of my neurotypical family members. However, I do not have a choice of which long-term memories I can remember; it seems to be a select few which are fairly random! It is worth mentioning that this will not be the case for all autistic ADHDers, but a fair few of us will have differences in our ability to process long-term memories compared to short-term memories.

EDUCATION, WORK AND HOME

If we take the example of our short-term memory and think about how many verbal instructions a teacher will likely give – or our boss at work while completing tasks on the go – we may be already disadvantaged at this point if we can't follow ten instructions that were only given once at lightning speed. In school, if we ask a teacher to repeat the instruction, we may get accused of deliberately not listening and teachers may incorrectly assume it's 'bad behaviour' or 'being naughty', when the reality is the teaching methods may not have been neurodivergent friendly. If we think about the university environment too and you attend a lecture that is not recorded, then you may miss out on noting down some information the lecturer was discussing due to the pace of the delivery, and afterwards we do not know how significant that information could have been for an upcoming exam or an essay.

While studying for my psychology degree, a paper that really stood out to me was one which found that short-term memory ability was strongly associated with academic success in school in the UK (Gathercole et al., 2004). So your full range of talents, qualities and true abilities may not be reflected in current educational assessments if you have difficulties with short-term memory and the right adjustments are not put in place by your school college or university. As autistic ADHDers are likely to experience challenges with short-term memory, this may apply to many of us, and can be one of the reasons why many of us do not get on well with school (to put it politely).

At work, it is highly unlikely that we'd be labelled as 'naughty' if we asked somebody to repeat or clarify; however, sometimes this might be met with hostility or people making incorrect assumptions about your job performance, when actually you are just asking so that you can perform well in your job. Interaction is always a two-way street, so when colleagues communicate tasks or requests it is best to establish a system which does not rely on your short-term memory as much, or at all.

Meanwhile, the nature of our jobs will often determine how much of our short-term memory we will need to use. Looking back on the jobs I have had so far, I have found that all of them place some level of demands on my short-term memory, but in very different ways. For example, my first job was working at a kids' after-school club and most instructions were communicated verbally, which was fine if there were only one or two, but if it was busy there could be a lot more, which was challenging on my short-term memory. In contrast now I work from home and have most instructions and tasks written down via email which is helpful, although keeping track of the ten tabs open on my computer and which one I need to use right now can take a lot of effort.

Ultimately it will be the balance between your short-term memory abilities and the short-term memory demands of your job that will dictate how challenging you may find a workplace. As no two work environments are ever exactly the same, there won't be one straightforward solution for keeping track of everything required when working or studying (which we will go through shortly).

Our short-term memory can affect us in many ways at home too.

Sometimes it can be the small things such as misplacing your phone and keys; the time when I left my keys in my fridge after getting back from doing the shopping is one example. However, this can cause more significant issues, like the time I misplaced my passport when living abroad – never to be seen again – which turned into a very expensive and bureaucratic long process to resolve!

Along with misplacing objects, having short-term memory difficulties can also make it hard to keep track of all the tasks we need to do around our home, such as cleaning, washing and planning our weekly meals. If we do manage to keep on top of the household tasks, it can often be super draining on our energy to the point where we spend all of our free time resting or our ability to engage with our interests and keep on top of other commitments is affected. It is important to find strategies that can work for us so we can try to avoid ending up in this situation.

Unlike many other 'tips and tricks' that are apparently written for autistic ADHDers, I am not going to recommend lists or trying to use your calendar as many neurotypicals do. First because you have likely been told this a million times already, and second if writing a list or using your calendar works for you, then chances are you are not seeking other solutions. Although I do find using an electronic calendar helps on a personal level with my organisation at work and home, it is certainly not the whole solution, as I still sometimes forget to add things to my calendar!

Something to always consider when people are trying to advise you on anything related to your autism and ADHD is how much do they know about autism and/or ADHD? If they are advising under the assumption that we function exactly like a neurotypical then it will likely not be very helpful for us, however well-intentioned they may be. One autistic ADHDer explained situations like this beautifully using the analogy of going fishing with the wrong tools.

> It's kind of like trying to fish but with a rope realising that, 'oh, I need a fishing rod'. Yeah. It's, it's like, well, fishing is easy for everybody. 'You just, you know, throw the thing out and you catch the fish', but what actually if you don't have the right or same tools, or you don't know the right things, of course, it's going to be tough. And you have to learn to adapt and find those, those things that aren't necessarily what most people would think of would help.

Now that we're aware that we should not accept advice from just anybody about things relating to being neurodivergent, let's get back to possible solutions for issues related to short-term memory! Firstly having instructions and important information written down as well as verbally communicated can be helpful, as you will always have a point of reference to check what is being asked of you, whether that is in school, at work or on your fridge at home. In educational settings, this doesn't have to be the teacher or lecturer writing it down specifically for you and handing it out (which many assume is the only way to accommodate students' needs). They can take what is referred to as a 'whole class approach' where they will write the instructions on the white board or a PowerPoint slide so that all students can benefit from the adjustment as well, which could be particularly helpful for other students who are not aware of their own neurodivergence yet. The benefit of teachers and lecturers taking this approach is that if you do not want other students knowing what your access needs are, this is a way to ensure your privacy is respected.

Similar to school, at work we are often given multiple instructions to follow at once, and sometimes at a pace where we cannot process everything that is being asked of us. For some having tasks communicated only verbally or only written down may be enough. However, those of us who need more could ask for adjustments, such as in how written tasks are formatted in an email (think bullet points, use of colour, headings or tables). I am also aware of some autistic ADHDers who are fans of using sticky notes on their walls or desk, so that the reminder is always there, and reducing the opportunity for their mind to wander and forget what they need to get done! Others prefer having reminders from colleagues to keep on track, and I definitely rely on this during times when my workload is higher than usual!

For those of us who decide to pursue higher education, universities are increasingly recording their lectures, which can be a life saver for those of us who can't rely on our short-term memories, as we can go back and watch the lecture as many times as we need to learn. Also, receiving the slides in advance can be helpful as often all the core information is written down, reducing the notes you will need to make as the teacher or lecturer is speaking so you can primarily focus on what they are saying, rather than trying to write everything down within a short space of time. I find that whether slides are shared in advance often comes down to each individual lecturer (and whether they remember), so you may want to send them a friendly reminder if you need this accommodation.

Though the workplace can be better, as agenda and meeting

minutes are common (so most things are written down), these are often just a summary and still may miss out key details that you need to do your job. Additionally, having challenges with short-term memory can make it more difficult to keep track of everything that is being said, which is why having the ability to record the audio from meetings can be an essential adjustment, so you can listen back or go over key points which were raised.

Some of the strategies we've mentioned for work and school can also be applied to managing home life, such as having written reminders where we need them. Some people do this by having a noticeboard and sticky notes to remind them of what they need to do around their home. Others may also label cupboards if their short-term memory affects their ability to remember where everything is kept in their home. However, this may create more challenges for some, as it is entirely possible that you might put something back in the wrong place without realising and then be unable to find it when it is not in the expected place! So often it is about figuring out what is going to work best for you.

If you share your household with others, then sometimes having people to remind you of what needs to be done or help you find misplaced items can be really helpful. If you live alone, it will perhaps be necessary to find other ways to be reminded of tasks. Personally, I use apps which send me notifications to keep on top of what needs to be done around the home, as I don't like being told what to do by other people in my home. However, some autistic ADHDers may need more support in this area, and if this is the case, it is worth exploring options of accessing social care in your local area. I am also aware of some autistic ADHDers who have set up accountability groups among themselves to send reminders in a non-judgemental way.

Impulsivity

Impulsivity is acting in the moment as a thought occurs in your mind, rather than thinking about something before acting on it. Sometimes professionals may also refer to impulsivity as lacking inhibition or inhibition control. However, impulsivity is not something that can always be controlled by an individual, and taking more impulsive actions than most is commonly associated with ADHD.

Being impulsive might include saying something out loud as soon as you think of it, being unable to wait until later on in a conversation when there is a natural pause. Some neurodivergent people have to say things as they think of them otherwise they will forget, and will consequently miss communicating something important. For some this will happen primarily because of their impulsivity, while others will say it's an element of both impulsivity and not wanting to forget to communicate important information. Other examples of impulsivity may include spending more money than you had planned and only realising when it is too late, or jumping into activities without thinking things through before you start (this could be either a positive or a negative thing depending on the activity).

As an autistic ADHDer, how can impulsivity manifest in daily life? I believe in many ways, and this is one of the key areas autism and ADHD can disguise each other. A common stereotype is that autistic people 'don't like change', or need everything planned to the nth degree to enjoy doing an activity. While that may be true for some autistics, if we are also ADHDers, then we may have a very different experience. Autistic ADHDers may like and even seek the need for change at times, which can be due to the impulsivity of ADHD. A classic example is when it comes to interests. Many autistics have interests which provide them with joy that often lasts for a long period of time. Autistic ADHDers, in contrast, may experience the same joy but find that it can be short lived, or that interests change quickly due to our impulsive nature. On a personal level, I have a few select interests that have stood the test of time, but I have lost track of the many others that have come and gone over the years!

Another example of how impulsivity can impact our experiences is with routines. It is often assumed that autistic people love routine while ADHD people cannot stick to one without support. So what does the relationship with routine mean for autistic ADHDers? It is a good question and it is likely to vary to some degree for each individual. However, many autistic ADHDers do feel the need for routine on some level, but can find it hard to follow. For some autistic ADHDers it could be that they do not need as in-depth or precise a routine as autistic people do, and they may need a lot of support or guidance to complete the routine. Again this example demonstrates that autistic ADHDers' experiences do not always (or even often) fit the stereotypes of how autism and ADHD present separately, but they both can influence how autistic ADHDers experience routines, which is not always acknowledged by professionals or those doing autism and ADHD assessments.

On a personal level, I do have some routines I need to follow such as my skincare routine, and some things I need to keep the same, e.g. the food I eat. However, many areas of my life are not like this, and some of my best memories have come from being spontaneous, which I credit to my impulsivity from my ADHD. So it is not all bad, even if at times being impulsive does create challenges in a world that is very neurotypical. I do find I am more likely to enjoy being spontaneous if there are no expectations put on me and I am in an environment where I can simply be myself.

EDUCATION, WORK AND HOME

Many educational institutions are not sympathetic to those of us with impulsive natures. People often wrongly assume that when we say something out loud or answer a question without raising our hands we are being rude, but the reality is often that we need to say what we're thinking straight away (otherwise we may forget).

Now if you are still in a school-like environment then I am going to give some advice that teachers may not like (but too bad!). Fidgeting is not just good, it is essential – many of us need the opportunity to fidget and stim while we concentrate. So while a teacher may view it as being defiant, I have heard from many autistic ADHDers that fidgeting during a class or lecture was their way of focusing their mind so they could take in what was being said. If they did not fidget or stim, then they could not engage. The same is true for me, as I was always doodling or fidgeting with a small object like a pen lid to focus. It's something I did instinctively and I remember having to do it subtly so I did not draw the attention of teachers, otherwise they would have made me stop and made the wrong assumptions.

When it comes to people's views on attention, I believe a cultural shift within education is needed where everyone understands that looking like you are focusing is not the same as actually focusing, to reduce the marginalisation neurodivergent people experience in education. Hopefully you will be in an understanding school or college, but if not, then you and/or your parents may need to speak to school staff such as the SENDCo (special educational needs coordinator) or your teachers about why you need these accommodations.

In contrast, at university, I found lecturers will not be focusing on whether you are fidgeting (as it is different from school where there is a much greater focus on behaviour), so this is less likely to be something you need to advocate for – or if you do, it may just be quickly explaining to the teacher or taking quick breaks from lectures and tutorials to stim.

For some autistic ADHDers in a school setting or a work meeting, instantly writing down their response may be helpful, so that their impulsive thoughts are still expressed (before they forget) and can be shared later on. However, teaching staff in schools and colleagues at work need to be understanding when autistic ADHDers do respond instantly. Ideally, others would acknowledge the person's impulsive contribution in the moment, and work out if that is the best time to discuss it, or find time later in the meeting or group discussion. This could look like somebody saying: 'Great point raised, we'll be able to address it fully in about ten minutes if that is okay?'

Having an impulsive nature can be interesting in the workplace, as it can either be a strength or weakness depending on the nature of our roles or simply what we need to get done that day. In roles where I have needed to use critical thinking abilities, impulsivity can be helpful as I bounce ideas around in my mind and explore different possibilities with my hyperactive thoughts. However, if my brain is experiencing impulsivity then having to sit down doing a repetitive task for hours on end can be impossible. My mind wanders, my body feels like it needs to move and it can go against my very nature to sit still just doing one task.

For those whose impulsivity requires them to move, movement breaks during the working day, classes and exams are an adjustment that should be granted too. You can ask for this adjustment if you feel it will help with your learning, being able to manage work and your ability to access education.

For some of us, our impulsive nature means our needs aren't always in sync with our educational and/or work demands. There are several options that we will go through next, but one that has come out top in discussions with fellow autistic ADHDers is flexible working and learning. I am fortunate enough to have this option now in my employed work, as I have a set number of hours I work a week, but a degree of flexibility in when these hours need to be during the week. And for my self-employed work, I have complete autonomy of when I work which is ideal!

However, it is important to acknowledge that not every job offers flexible hours, and at the time of writing it is often a privilege to have flexible working or learning hours. In an ideal world, it would be the norm for both work and educational providers to offer flexible hours and ways of work. Unfortunately, for the vast majority of jobs I have worked over the years, there was no option for flexible working and as a consequence I did not last in any of these jobs for longer than a year. The combination of flexible working hours and working from home has been the solution for me in terms of sustaining employment, and sustaining employment can be challenging to do if we are impulsive. I am not saying flexible working environments are the solution for all autistic ADHDers who experience impulsivity, but it can make a big difference for some of us. If this level of flexibility was standard across employers, I do think that the employment issues autistic ADHDers experience would be reduced. It has been great to see remote working become a more widely available option in recent years; I hope this will extend to education too, as school, colleges and university environments are not always accessible for us.

So for autistic ADHDers who currently do not have flexibility working or learning, we do need understanding from those around us. One example may be that our ability to do certain tasks may fluctuate during the day depending on our impulsivity. It may be a case of speaking with your employer or educational provider about how impulsivity works and how they can allocate certain tasks accordingly or try and give you a timetable that works around the times where you may be more likely to be impulsive. For example, you may find you are more impulsive in the morning, so doing more repetitive tasks may be better for you in the afternoon. Alternatively, you may explain that your impulsivity can be unpredictable, so it is best to have regular conversations about what you can do on each day.

Our impulsive natures can also affect us at home. We may find that we struggle to complete tasks when we have the time to do them, but then have a sudden burst of energy to get on top of the housework during times we are super busy or need to follow through on other commitments. Some people also describe this as if they are driven by a motor and their body goes into autopilot – although this does not happen all the time! For many autistic ADHDers who experience this, it tends to happen at unpredictable moments, which is why it can create challenges if we feel driven by a motor when we want to be doing something else.

Not every one of us experiences these bursts of energy and focus, and for some autistic ADHDers, it is certainly the case that managing home life is always challenging due to impulsivity. It may be that some of us may need additional support or rely on others to help manage and keep up with household-related tasks, which is entirely understandable. Some autistic ADHDers rely on apps and other technology to help prompt them to do certain tasks, while others will block out certain times in the week to try and get tasks done. Others still accept that their house will be messy to some degree, but focus on keeping on top of the essentials, as that is all they can manage. As you can see, there isn't one solution and it's often a case of trial and error to find what works for you.

For me personally, I can only keep on top of housework if I have nothing else to do, and as I work full time, this is certainly somewhat challenging for me. I have to accept that I need to rely on others to get all the household tasks done. For me (and I suspect many other autistic ADHDers), the biggest challenge can be managing the combined demands of work and home life, while having an impulsive nature. Although the tips and tricks I've learnt over the years and have shared in this chapter can be enough support for some autistic ADHDers, some will need support from others as well.

Some autistic ADHDers decide to take medication if their impulsivity becomes too much of a barrier for their home and work lives or education. Going on ADHD medication should always be a personal choice, and nobody should be pressured by others to take medication. However, some of those who do decide to try ADHD medication find it makes a positive difference for them. My advice to anybody who is considering this option is to speak with an understanding doctor you can trust, so that you can decide if medication is the best option for you, and if so, which medication, as there are usually several options. Also you should not feel pressured into continuing to take it if it is not right for you, or the side effects are not worth any benefits you may get from taking the medication. As I have not tried ADHD medication myself, I spoke with several autistic ADHDers for this book who shared their experiences of ADHD medication.

> I will say as well since being on ADHD medication, my autistic side is a lot more obvious because I don't have to deal so much and can focus on things a lot more. I rarely get overwhelmed by things on my medication because it's like, I haven't got all of the thoughts happening that would normally distract me from it.

It is also worth remembering that for some of us, we may have to try a few different forms of ADHD medication (as there are several) until we find the right one for us.

> Making sure that you've tried all the different avenues and also realising if actually this isn't working for me (the medication) or this is like causing a side effect that's not worth it.

If we have negative side effects, we do not have to continue with the medication (it is not a life and death situation!). The medication is supposed to improve our quality of life, and if it doesn't, then we do not have to take it. Another autistic ADHDer I spoke with shared the difficulties they had with ADHD medication.

66 My ADHD has been resistant to most medications, so I've gone through most of my life completely untreated.

So as you can see, just because we are all autistic ADHDers, does not mean that we will have identical experiences or the same benefits from taking medication. It is a very individual choice, including how our mind and bodies may also respond to medication. The most important thing is that we speak with the right medical professionals who have knowledge about ADHD medication if it is something we wish to try.

Task switching, initiation and autistic inertia

Task initiation and switching describes somebody's ability to either start a new task and to finish one task and then start another within a relatively short space of time. For some people task switching or starting a task is something that they do without thinking about it. However, for many autistic ADHDers starting a task and/or switching to a different task can take a lot of mental effort. If we think back to monotropism in the previous chapter, often our brains can hyper-focus on singular activities meaning anything that disturbs our natural flow state is disorientating. This is especially true in the modern world where everything seems to be more fast-paced, and task switching seems to happen more frequently and quickly.

If you find task switching or initiation harder, then you may need to save your daily energy for just shopping or socialising for a few hours, rather than trying to fit everything into a shorter period of time (for example, spending an hour doing cleaning, then an hour going out to the shops and the next hour socialising with friends), which our neurotypical society often expects everyone can do automatically.

In older medical descriptions of autism, this was often described as 'resistance to change' or 'insistence on routines'. However, on a personal level I have never felt these descriptions captured neurodivergent people's reality and were often based on assumptions that neurotypicals made from just observing neurodivergent people, rather than understanding our internal experiences in an authentic way. The use of terms such as 'resistant' and 'insistent' makes it sound as if it is an intentional bad choice we are making, which is certainly not the case here!

A more recent description of what some autistic ADHDers may experience is called 'autistic inertia'. Autistic inertia essentially describes the tendency to stay focused on one task, and difficulties related to task switching (Autistic Inertia, 2022). Even if somebody wants to start or switch to an activity they enjoy, sometimes they cannot due to autistic inertia and feeling stuck on the task or activity they are currently on (this can also apply to starting the day and getting out of bed in the morning). So, for example, even if I really want to play *The Sims* (which is my favourite computer game), sometimes I cannot due to autistic inertia, as it is too much mental effort for my brain to stop what I am currently doing and then follow the steps needed to go to my laptop and load up the game. On the flip side, if I am really into my game to the point where I am hyper-focused, then stopping the activity and interrupting my focus can sometimes be incredibly difficult due to autistic inertia. Autistic inertia may not be present every time you switch between an activity or try and stop a task, but many autistic people, including autistic

ADHDers, experience it often enough to acknowledge that it is a frequent challenge they face in daily life.

Also, it can feel like a struggle to organise my thoughts in my head so I can process all the steps involved to play *The Sims*, which is where I believe the ADHD comes in and adds an additional layer to how I experience autistic inertia. So although autistic inertia is a concept that seeks to explain the experiences of autistic people, ADHD may also affect how autistic ADHDers experience inertia, as some of us seek variety in terms of what we're doing. Some of us may not experience inertia to the same degree, or experience it less frequently than autistic people who are also not ADHDers. Some may have periods where they experience a lot more autistic inertia than others. As autistic inertia is a topic that has only just started to be spoken about recently, it is still not yet fully understood; however, I am fairly confident that we will all have our own unique experiences with it (like with most things related to our neurodivergence).

EDUCATION, WORK AND HOME

Task switching is common in a lot of workplaces and educational settings to some degree, but it could massively vary depending on what your job involves or how your school, college or university operates. One way to get an indication of whether task switching will be a big part of a job is to read the job description and see how many different core tasks are mentioned. If you are moving on to a new college or university, it is worth asking what a timetable may look like to anticipate the amount of task switching that may be required throughout the day, to judge if it is the right learning environment for you. Also, if you are in a job interview, it is always worth asking what a typical or average day would be like in the role, as this will give an indication of how much task switching there will likely be.

For some autistic ADHDers, having a variety of tasks to do throughout the day will suit them well due to the novelty-seeking that can come with ADHD, so a job that switches between tasks can work well for some of us. Others may experience difficulties with jobs of this nature because it can take significant mental effort to be constantly moving from one task to another. On a personal level, I do think that my ADHD has a role to play here as I like regularly moving from one thing to the next (rather than continually doing the same task), but my autism means that I have a specific way of switching tasks that works for me.

With home life, we may have a lot more control or autonomy over our time and how things are managed, meaning that we can transition between tasks and activities in a way that works for us most of the time. However, if you have pets, children or other significant responsibilities at home this will obviously be different. Although I am not a parent of a human child, I am fully aware that my cat and fur baby Milo would not be happy if I didn't feed him when he was hungry because I was in the middle of doing something. He definitely wouldn't wait until I was ready to feed him, he would not leave me alone until I did! So naturally, I do have to transition from doing one task to another at home to meet Milo's needs, and I'd imagine this would be even more the case if you have a child. On the plus side, I am aware roughly of when Milo will be wanting food, so I can plan to some degree when I am likely to be interrupted. Once you've been responsible for another being for some time, generally speaking there will be a routine established. So although this may be hard in the beginning, over time it often becomes easier.

In daily life, it would be ideal for some of us if there was not constant switching all the time (although some of us may love the novelty of something new). However, there are some things that can help make it easier with task switching if we find it difficult. One example would be pre-warning for changes, which could be as simple as an app or another person reminding you when an upcoming change or transition is happening, giving you a few minutes to mentally prepare for the change rather than being expected to manage the change on the spot with no warning. How understanding our colleagues are can also make a big difference, as they may or may not assume everybody can switch between different activities at a moment's notice. We may need to explain adjustments to employers and educational institutions, so we can have as much notice as possible of any changes.

I have also heard of people leaving a few minutes early from a meeting/class in a busy work or educational setting to avoid key transition times, avoiding the sensory overload of several hundred other people moving between rooms at once and allowing more time to manage each change throughout the day. Also if I have a busy day of meetings, I try to make sure that I have at least some time in between each (about 15 minutes), as I struggle with instant task switching; having that breathing space allows me to mentally prepare to change my focus.

One autistic ADHDer opened up about how having better understanding of their ADHD helped them to work out how they could start tasks.

> **Right now yeah, I am probably not struggling with it myself as much. Whereas before, I would tell myself, I'm lazy and I just couldn't be bothered. Whereas now I know I'm dopamine**

deficient, and find, you know, maybe if I have some dark chocolate or do some stretches or just move my body around for like 10–20 minutes, it will give me enough dopamine to then mean that I can motivate myself to go and do that task that I didn't want to go and do before. Yeah, it's just sort of learning to be more accepting of the challenges that I face. That's what's really helped.

There is a theory that having lower dopamine (a chemical in the body) levels is why ADHDers may seek novelty or can struggle with motivation (Levy, 1991). So for this autistic ADHDer, the key is finding ways to boost their dopamine levels to help them to start tasks they could not find the motivation to start initially.

When it comes to organisation in general, another autistic ADHDer I spoke with shared what has helped them manage daily tasks, and the importance of recognising how our energy levels can also impact our ability to carry them out:

66 Planning and organising is something I've gotten a lot better at as I've gotten older – if I'm given much more time than other people would typically need. I've noticed that 'simple' tasks, things which take other people very little time or energy, turn out to be complicated undertakings for me; I need to break them down into smaller steps, AND factor in the time that I'll get distracted or need to take breaks so I won't get bored.

As doing tasks which involve executive functioning can take a lot more energy for us (compared to neurotypical people), it is important that we do factor in any breaks and the amount of time we need to complete the task, as this will likely differ. In

Chapter 3, 'Adulthood and decision making', we will also look at additional strategies that can help with understanding our energy levels, and how we can manage this on a daily basis.

Sequencing

Sequencing is an executive function that is not talked about by professionals as much as the previous three we've explored, but it is something many autistic ADHDers can be affected by daily. Sequencing is the order of steps somebody follows to complete a task. Now I cannot say this for certain, as I am an autistic ADHDer myself, but apparently neurotypicals can follow steps in the intended order to complete a task without significant effort (shocking I know!).

Although differences in sequencing are usually associated with ADHD, they are certainly present in autistic ADHDers too, and I believe that the sequencing differences for many autistic ADH-Ders go against the stereotypes of autism. Similarly to impulsivity, not following an exact order or routine for everything may seem not very autistic-like. Even if an autistic ADHDer has a set routine they need or would like to follow, they may jump from one task to another in an order that may not seem logical to others. Sometimes this can make sense for that individual autistic ADHDer, especially if they are in a flow-like state while completing an activity. However, the opposite can also be true where some autistic ADHDers may have a strong need to follow a routine in a certain way, but due to their difficulties they have with their sequencing, it can feel impossible for them to achieve. Alternatively, they may struggle with the organisational side of following a routine. So as you can see, even though we all may be autistic ADHDers, there is no 'one size fits all' approach in terms of how we experience our neurodivergence and sequencing of tasks.

Typical sequencing

Sequencing for some autistic ADHDers

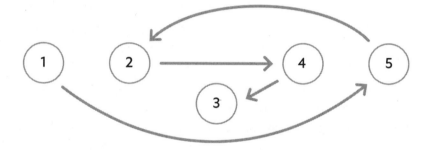

Sequencing is something that I experience due to my hyperactive thoughts. I find that I will start the first step of a task, but my mind wanders to the fifth step, so I start doing the fifth step. I will do this for a while until I realise that I actually needed to finish steps 1, 2, 3 and 4 to be able to do step 5 well, but often I cannot remember what I need to do for the previous steps without a reminder due to my short-term memory difficulties. On the previous page is a diagram comparing how I see sequencing can often work for neurotypicals compared to autistic ADHDers (and for some other neurodivergent people too).

Being in a world that assumes we all have a typical style of thinking can certainly cause additional challenges for us autistic ADHDers, as almost everything is communicated in the style of following certain steps in a certain order, without consideration that it may not be the only way to achieve a task or goal. Often at school and work people will be expected to follow typical sequencing styles of thinking, and if our teachers or colleagues do not have the understanding of neurodivergence, then this can put us at a disadvantage. Having understanding from the people around us is vital, but also having adjustments in place such as written reminders can help when our brains start to jump from one step to another; others find that ADHD medication can help with this.

For myself, I see sequencing as both a blessing and a curse. Some of my most creative ideas have come from having hyperactive thoughts jumping from one topic to another, but it is less convenient when I need to do tasks such as cleaning or doing the laundry. If I am being truly honest, I'm experiencing hyperactive thoughts while writing this paragraph, which is impacting my sequencing in writing and structuring my ideas.

EDUCATION, WORK AND HOME

Many educational settings and work settings often expect everyone to complete tasks following a prescribed sequence, and often without much flexibility (even though in many cases at least, some level of flexibility is possible). If either educational institutions or employers are not willing to find alternative solutions, then by default they create spaces that are inaccessible for many autistic ADHDers. Often autistic ADHDers are blamed for their differences causing the problem, without any consideration of what changes could be made to create an inclusive environment. So the big question is, what can schools, colleges, universities and employers do to become more accessible for those who do not sequence in a typical way?

A lot of the time, educators and employers will often correct others to follow a typical sequencing style by default, without realising that it may not be accessible to them. Ideally, rather than correcting us automatically to use a neurotypical way of thinking, those we work with should be curious about our approaches to problem solving and finding out the answers. We may not necessarily be going down the wrong path, just one that does not look like the one they anticipated us following. You never know, we may even teach them a thing or two about how we approach tasks!

However, for some of us our brain's sequencing process can be debilitating and act as a barrier to our learning or maintaining a job. It may be like this throughout our lives, or may only be debilitating in certain situations. If this is the case, then we will need adjustments so we can have access to the same education and work opportunities. Additionally, it can also be helpful to speak with members of your team or manager about what is the best way for them to communicate tasks. The type of adjustments needed will vary depending on the individual person's needs. For some this may be having written reminders of how they should carry out a task, whereas others may use visual reminders or a combination of both.

Apps and technology can also be useful to help plan out our sequencing. Again these reminders could be right in front of you on your desk or somewhere else in the room where everyone can see them. I mainly use apps to help me organise my to-do list in an order that makes sense to me. These apps give me the option to change the order with one click, something that is not so easy to do with pen and paper without making things look too disorganised to understand later. They are a tool I started using while studying in university that have worked well for me, to the extent that it's now part of my daily life while managing both work and home commitments.

For some of us autistic ADHDers, our ability to follow a sequence and complete tasks can be influenced by the environment we are in, and we may need to consider if there are any sensory-related needs that are making things more difficult for us. So a sensory audit (examination of potential sensory triggers in a room) may be needed for classrooms, lecture halls or the workplace so that necessary adjustments can be made accordingly. If you experience barriers when advocating for your needs in this way, or you are not comfortable with face-to-face learning and working, then it is always worth asking about online learning options and working from home. If you feel that the sensory environment of classrooms and offices may be too much or distracting, then you may choose to study where courses can be facilitated entirely online and seek jobs which are entirely working from home. Although working from home can be a lifeline for some autistic ADHDers in terms of accessing work and education, for others it can be detrimental. As one autistic ADHDer put it:

> 66 I cannot work from home because home is for home stuff. Yeah, same with high school. I can't do homework at home. Because home is for hobbies, for fun stuff.

Having clear boundaries between work, education and home

is essential for some of us, so working from home isn't always an option. In that case, adjusting the sensory environment at home or working and studying in an environment where you do not get overwhelmed (that is not home) could be the best options. Sometimes it may be a case of working or studying in a different room in the building. If it becomes a significant issue for you, to the point it is impacting your ability to do your job or access education, then it may be worth having a conversation with your educational provider or workplace. I am aware that this can be a difficult issue to raise, so we will cover this later on when looking at 'Your needs at work' (Chapter 3), and 'Work and mental health' (Chapter 5).

Some autistic ADHDers may also need more time than others anticipate to complete a task or follow a sequence. One of the autistic ADHDers I spoke with while writing this book shared the importance of educational settings providing adjustments for this:

> Homework always took me three times as long as the 'recommended time' teachers assumed we'd need, and I never had time for extracurriculars as a result.

And also added:

> Almost every task, no matter how seemingly small it is, has to be broken down into tiny steps for me or I won't fully understand how to do it.

Another autistic ADHDer I spoke with also opened up about how the flexibility of their workplace means they are able to work in a way that suits them best, and means they can follow a sequence of tasks in the best way for their brain:

> **"** Luckily, when it comes to work, I am really grateful for my job because I kind of pick and choose what I do and when I do it. So my manager just gives me a whole bunch of tasks and he's like, do these in whatever order you want. You can start on one, go to three, go back to one, then like start on the fourth. And it's just, it's brilliant because I can just pick and choose what I feel like doing on that day.

In an ideal world, we would have the flexibility to work in the best way for us, as it means we can do our actual job to the best of our ability, rather than having to focus on doing the job in a neurotypical way (which takes up so much more of our energy and can contribute to burnout). So if you are an employer or work in HR and are reading this, take note!

Having additional time, flexibility with how we complete our work, and accommodations in how tasks are communicated to us (such as being broken down step by step) are just some examples of ways to help us to engage with our education or work, giving us a better opportunity to demonstrate our full abilities.

One adjustment which I found made a big difference in terms of being able to follow a sequence was the use of a flow chart. The nature of one particular task meant that I had to follow a sequence in a specific order and I was having difficulties following this process, as it was assumed I could follow the task using the instructions that all of my neurotypical colleagues were able to follow. However, I could not follow them relying only on verbal instructions. So creating a flow chart with my manager at the time helped me to keep on track and avoid making the same mistakes repeatedly.

Below is a template of what a flow chart may look like, with one instruction in each box. These can be helpful for a variety of situations such as making phone calls, carrying out administration tasks and following important regulations (that may be applicable to your job). You could also adapt this template to add more or fewer boxes depending on the sequence you need to follow.

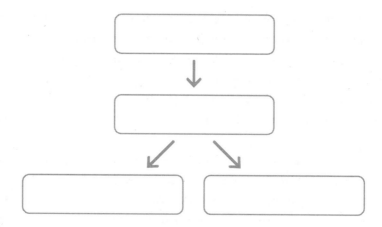

A flow chart doesn't have to be limited to just a work environment. It can also be a helpful tool for getting household tasks done or for following all the steps required to complete the coursework for a module you may be studying. It's often a case of trying it out to see if it works for any tasks you may need to complete in a certain order.

With home life, there can be less pressure to follow sequences in terms of keeping up with cleaning, washing and cooking. In some ways this can be a blessing, as we have more freedom to sequence in a way that suits us at home. Although for some, this may mean that some tasks get delayed to the point where they can cause issues, e.g. running out of clean clothes and having to do a quick dash to the shops to buy some more (yes, this has happened to me more than once). At this point we may need to either reach out for support with completing tasks or finding a specific strategy to help keep on top of tasks (like those mentioned above).

If we live with people who are not understanding, this can also create additional challenges. When I previously lived with family and in house shares, there was pressure to keep up with the neurotypical way of sequencing, due to sharing living spaces needing to always be kept clean (so others could also use communal spaces such as the kitchen). Often I need to take a break between finishing cooking and washing up due to managing my energy levels throughout the day, and other autistic ADHDers may have difficulties with following through due to their sequencing differences. In these situations we may need to have conversations with the people we live with to find a solution that works for everyone (ideally). Still, if the people we live with are unwilling to understand the difficulties we are experiencing then it may be necessary to either explore options for accessing additional support (e.g. social care/disability support in your area) or even reconsidering your living situation (if possible – this is worst-case scenario and hopefully it won't come to this!).

Time blindness

Our differences in executive functioning in the areas of impulsivity, task switching and sequencing may contribute to us experiencing something called 'time blindness' which is often associated with ADHD. Time blindness is when people (mainly ADHDers) struggle with having a sense of time when it comes to completing tasks and activities throughout the day. As a result we may be running late all the time, or leave things to the last minute without intentionally doing so. For example, we may miss the bus to school or work because we got distracted by social media on our phones or the TV during our morning routines (this has happened to me more than once!).

Although time blindness may not be something you have experienced, as we become older and more independent, we often become more responsible for managing our time, meaning we experience the impact of time blindness for the first time as young adults. So the question is, what can help with time blindness?

EDUCATION, WORK AND HOME

In terms of the strategies people can use to help with time blindness, some people try to do things in advance, to avoid the risk of running out of time in the future. An example might be preparing your lunch the evening before you have school, college, university or work, rather than doing it as part of your morning routine. Having a few less things to do in the morning means that if you are starting to run late with your morning routine, it will be less likely to have an impact on the rest of your day (as there will be fewer things you need to do before a certain time).

A similar tool that can help some autistic ADHDers with time blindness is aiming to get something done before the deadline or arriving before the time they are due to be somewhere. This is often what I do, as I like to have the comfort of knowing that if I start running late for something, I have some 'cushioning time', where even if I am running a bit late, I will still get there by the time I need to be there. I just won't be as early as I thought I may have been. This is why I am always super early if I have a certain train to catch or if I am flying out of an airport.

Also having cues in our lives can help us keep on track if we struggle with time blindness. One example is having visual reminders where we need them to do certain tasks (e.g. having a sticky note on the fridge of all the tasks you need to do in the kitchen during the morning and/or evening), or using tools such as flow charts mentioned above, if they are helpful for keeping track of time as well as the things we need to do. Cues to help us keep track of time don't just have to be visual either! We can use things such as timers, alarms and notifications on our phones to help remind us when to do tasks at certain points throughout the day. If you have somebody you trust enough, you can also ask them to remind you of certain things or keep track of time. It is all about finding what works best for you.

If a workplace has flexible working hours, this can be a great lifeline, as if we are running late, it gives us the flexibility to start work later than usual, or we can work at a time that is easier for us. If this would make a big difference for you, then it is worth looking for employers that offer flexible working or ask for it as an adjustment. Also in schools and education environments, an adjustment some autistic people have is leaving their class a few minutes early, to avoid the sensory overwhelm of busy corridors when transitioning from one classroom to the next one – this accommodation could also work if you have time blindness as it can help you get to where you need to be at the right time! If you are struggling with time blindness in education or work and would like to ask for support, you can ask for the adjustments needed (including the ones mentioned above), as these strategies can all be incorporated and adapted in different environments.

DON'T FORGET!

If you are in education still, it is worth adding you may be able to access additional support for the duration of your studies (depending on where you are studying, and what stage of your education you are at). I found the additional support I received at university made a big difference in terms of being able to complete my studies. So I would highly recommend contacting the SEND department and/or disability support services where you are studying (or thinking of studying) to see what specific support you can access.

When you take into account other ways educational settings are not often accessible to autistic ADHDers, such as with sensory overload, navigating neurotypical social interaction and executive functioning, it is clear to see why many of us have negative and traumatic experiences in school. As you come to school-leaving age, it is entirely understandable if you want nothing more to do with the formal education system and need time to recover from it. There are other opportunities open to people that do not involve going into further or higher education, such as apprenticeships and entry-level jobs, which we will talk about more in the next chapter.

3
Adulthood and decision making

Coming into adulthood is an interesting phase as we are often faced with making big decisions for the first time during our lives and can have a million new responsibilities thrown our way. For some of us this is exciting, as we finally have the autonomy to make the decisions we want for ourselves and seek the freedom that comes with this. For others, it is a scary time due to worries of not being able to manage the new responsibilities we may have and coping with big life changes, along with potentially being overwhelmed with the number of upcoming choices we need to make.

These are all common worries among young people; however, as autistic ADHDers, there is often a lot more we need to take into consideration. Such as how are we going to pursue our goals and desires while trying not to burn out? If we decide to enter further education, how do we know if the support structures will be in place so we can thrive? Or if we want to go into a certain career, how accessible is it for us with our individual needs? Can we manage a full time job? Or is self-employment a better option? How am I going to keep on top of bills?

We will start off this chapter by going through the changes that can come with adulthood, which are relevant for everyone, and which many people just assume everybody knows. The problem with this is many autistic ADHDers do not have the 'how to survive as an adult' manual that our neurotypical society expects us to have (unhelpful, I know!). We will therefore go through some of the aspects of becoming an adult so that you won't have to learn the hard way, like many of us older autistic ADHDers had to previously.

It can also feel impossible to figure out how to make these big decisions everyone must make at the start of adulthood, which will vary for each autistic ADHDer. As I do not know everybody's individual circumstances, it would not be wise for me to simply state what I think the decisions are that all autistic ADHDers need to make (I'm not a fan of that approach anyway). However, what I do feel I can offer is different ideas and possibilities to think about when you have to make an important decision for the first time. Hopefully these questions can act as a starting point to figure out your choices on decisions that can feel impossible to make. If I am being honest, this neurotypical world does not always make it clear how to figure this stuff out, especially when you have to factor in your needs as a neurodivergent person.

Coming into adulthood when we are neurodivergent

I have had many conversations with fellow autistic ADHDers about the parts of adulthood which are important to know about, but never explained. In true neurodivergent style, I got many responses and ideas about what older autistic ADHDers would have liked to have known when they were young adults. As there were several similar themes that came up, we will go through these in this chapter, so that you can feel a little more ahead of the game than many of us did during our teens and early twenties.

Sometimes living up to 'adult expectations' feels impossible, because it is. Trust me, most adults actually have no idea what they are doing most of the time: they spend most of their time pretending they do (even the neurotypical ones) and it is impossible to know everything. Therefore, it's important to be aware of what we do know, what we don't know, and how to reach out for help/information in situations where we need to know something that we don't yet.

An example might be that you receive your first payslip and you don't understand all the information on there. In this situation, the person responsible for payroll (processing people's pay) at your work should be able to tell you what everything means if you ask. This can feel nerve racking in the moment, so you could also try to find your answer on Google.

Moving into my own place for the first time has definitely reminded me that it is not possible to do everything for myself (as well as not being able to know everything), e.g. putting together flat pack furniture isn't always possible alone, and I needed to get professional advice to figure out what budget I had and where I could afford to live. I find I naturally want to do everything myself due to my past experiences and being neurodivergent, but I have to accept that sometimes it is more beneficial to reach out for help in areas that are my weaknesses, where I cannot do it properly myself or do not have access to all the information needed to make informed choices.

Often during the early years of adulthood, many of us autistic ADHDers have felt doing all the same things as our neurotypical peers is a lot harder, and that's often because it is. Although there are strategies we can put in place to help manage the challenges of everyday life (more on that later), it can be incredibly hard to manage a job, be responsible for other people and/ or pets and manage home life.

Personally I remember feeling so overwhelmed when I first started working full time (with a long commute on top) about how I was going to manage this for the rest of my working life. The reality was I wasn't going to be able to. So although we can try and do all of the same things that neurotypicals can manage, it will likely feel a lot harder, and sometimes this can be at the cost of other things in our lives. This can also make important choices harder to make, as we may have fewer options when we factor in our own needs – when creating a life for ourselves that will work.

It's important to remember that this is not our fault (although we are often made to feel that way). I know saying this won't change the reality of daily life, but self-blame is often the last thing we need on top of everything else when life is difficult. Being an autistic ADHDer in this world is often hard, and it can be truly disabling for some of us. It has taken years (and is still a work in progress), but I can finally say I have created a life that suits me and my neurodivergent needs well, without feeling guilty about not living up to 'normal' standards. Getting this balance right hasn't been easy, and involved figuring out the balance of what

I can and cannot manage, what I can afford, and what things were going to make me happy in life. This might look different to what most other people would consider normal, but that is totally okay, as being 'normal' would only make my life miserable (more on that in Chapter 6!).

Recognising our neurodivergent needs

Being autistic ADHDers means that our needs are likely different from most others, so it is worth spending time recognising what these are and figuring out how they can be met. No matter how well-intentioned some neurotypical people may be, if their advice to you is generic, making blanket statements that they feel apply to all people, then chances are the advice given will not work for us, no matter how many times they insist a hot drink and warm bath will solve all of our problems (if only life were that easy!).

In terms of recognising our own needs, trying to manage our energy levels and avoiding burnout can often be a priority for many autistic ADHDers. Using tools such as the Spoon theory by Christine Miserandino (2003) can help in terms of recognising how much energy (represented by spoons) we have during the day, and planning out what we will be able to manage.

For example, you may start your day with ten spoons. Certain activities will take up a certain number of spoons:

- Social – three spoons.
- Studying – four spoons.
- Cooking and household tasks – three spoons.

As you can see, spoons can be used up fairly quickly and it is at this point you recognise that you cannot use any more without having a break or rest to regain your spoons (energy back). The good thing about the spoons concept is it can be very flexible, so if you find socialising particularly draining, then you can change it from three to say five spoons. Also depending on how much socialising you do, it may take up a different number of spoons day to day.

Another part of recognising your neurodivergent needs is understanding what gives us energy. This includes obvious things such as sleeping, naps and eating, but it can also be doing the things we enjoy – engaging in our interests being a key one! I also find doing exercise I enjoy such as bouncing and swimming gives me energy (although this definitely does not apply to all forms of exercise as I can't stand jogging/running).

Spoons theory is just one of many ways we autistic ADHDers can keep track of our energy. Many use similar concepts to the spoons, but with different analogies. For example, some autistic ADHDers may use a phone battery to represent their energy levels, with different daily activities taking up a certain percentage of their battery charge. Some also use colours or visual blocks to represent energy, as it can be easier to keep track of what they can manage using physical objects/visuals rather than concepts that can be a little more abstract (such as spoons). Others prefer using energy accounting by Maja Toudal (McKay 2020), where draining activities debit from and energising ones credit into our energy bank account, so they can recognise when they are about to go into the negative and run out of energy. Below is an example of what energy accounting can look like:

Activity	Credits	Debits
Sleep	100	
Work		60
Social		20
Cooking		10
Engaging in interests	30	
End of day balance	40	

Another important aspect for autistic ADHDers is meeting our sensory needs. Having the combination of sensory sensitivities from being autistic and being distracted by sensory stimuli from our ADHD can create sensory needs that need to be met so that we can be happy. As part of this, the first step is to identify your own sensory needs. You could do this by either thinking about and writing down what those needs are, or use one of the many sensory audit forms and questionnaires that are out there online that can help identify needs. However, if you are overwhelmed by where to even start, I have created the table on the next page that can help you to start to identify some of your sensory needs.

These questions are by no means an exhaustive list of all the possible sensory needs we may have, but are good questions to ask yourself to start working out what your sensory needs are, based on common ones many autistic people (including autistic ADHDers) have. Once you feel you have a good understanding of areas in your life where you may have sensory needs, next you should figure out how you can meet those needs. For example, getting noise cancelling earphones to reduce noise or avoiding

Sense	Hypersensitive	Hyposensitive
Sound	• Do sudden loud noises make you jump? • Do you have difficulties filtering out background noise? • Do you find noisy environments such as shops difficult to be in?	• Do you enjoy listening to certain sounds at louder levels? • Do you enjoy being in places with a lot of noise, e.g. concerts or festivals.
Taste	• Do you find the taste of certain foods makes you gag/feel sick? • Do you prefer bland foods over flavoured food?	• Do you need lots of flavour on your food to be able to eat it? • Do you need to mix lots of different types of food together to feel satisfied?
Touch	• Do you find certain textures of clothes too uncomfortable to wear? • Do you feel physically uncomfortable when people give you a hug? Or shake your hand?	• Do you need to feel certain materials to feel joy? • Do you enjoy deep pressure and feel the need to seek it out?
Smell	• Do common smells such as some food or fragrances make you feel sick? • Do you find that you can only manage and perhaps enjoy subtle smells such as vanilla?	• Do you have certain smells that you seek out and need a lot of to experience them, e.g. lavender or the smell of a bakery?

Sight	• Do you find certain lights and colours overwhelming? • Do you prefer having lights off, or dimmed to a level that most people would find too dark?	• Do you enjoy or feel fixated by spinning and moving objects? • Do you feel drawn to bright and/or flashing lights?
Balance (vestibular)	• Do you experience car sickness easily? • Do you experience a lot of dizziness after not much movement?	• Do you seek out the sensations from riding a fast rollercoaster or similar? • Do you need to spin or rock or do other stims?
Awareness of space (proprioception)	• Do you need a lot more personal space than most other people? • Do you find it difficult to know where/how you move your body in crowded spaces?	• Do you bump into objects frequently without realising? • Do you struggle to judge how much force/pressure is needed when doing physical activities?
Awareness of internal body signals (interoception)	• Are you always feeling hungry and/or thirsty? • Do you feel the need to go to the toilet, even if your bladder is empty?	• Do you not recognise toilet urges (until you really need to go)? • Do you struggle to recognise when you need to eat and drink without reminders?

the kitchen when others in your household are cooking food that is too overwhelming for your nose. One of the autistic ADHDers I spoke with opened up about the positive difference noise cancelling headphones had made for them:

66 It's like if I'm standing right next to speakers, I feel like I'm gonna pass out if it's emergency services (sirens), I just I can't stand it. I feel like I'm gonna fall over and that's where my noise cancelling headphones come into play. I love my noise cancelling headphones.

Also, I have noticed in recent years more peer support groups and systems have been set up by and for neurodivergent people. I often find that part of the reason for this is people discovering their neurodivergence (or just trying to understand it better) for the first time, and wanting to understand themselves better and find out how they can meet their neurodivergent needs. Peer support groups may not have all the answers, but they can be an incredibly useful resource to hear how people similar to us manage in their daily lives and feel less alone in a neurotypical world.

Managing money

One of the biggest changes we will have as adults is having full control over our finances. Up until now, you may have had access to small amounts of pocket money, or some money from doing odd jobs growing up. As adults, we will likely have access to more money, as well as additional responsibilities, such as making sure we can pay our bills on time and that we have enough to cover all of our essential costs.

The first time we take on this responsibility can feel like a bit of a shock, as we often have to set aside a certain amount of money to cover our essential costs for the first time (which is usually a reasonably large chunk of our income). When we were younger we may have been able to spend the small amount of money we had on what we liked without a second thought, but in adulthood we must work out how much money we have, how much is needed to pay bills, how much to save, and how much we can spend as we wish.

If you want to keep track of your money and your costs, you could create a spreadsheet, or use a table like the one below. I have given some examples of common monthly costs that you may have. Also the amounts below are just examples! These may vary significantly depending on your own personal situation and where you live. The table below is to demonstrate one way to keep track of spending if you have not done so before but need to now.

Essential bills	Money to spend on myself	Savings
• Rent – 500 • Food – 200 • Utility bills (water/ electricity/ gas) – 100 • Internet – 25 • Transport – 50	• Interests – 50 • Day trip out – 40 • Meal out – 10	• Savings Account – 100
Total: 875	100	100

Also, technology has progressed so that now some banks can provide a breakdown of where you are spending your money each month on their app. It may be worth checking if your bank has this feature or something similar, as it may save you some time rather than creating a table or setting up a spreadsheet.

As autistic ADHDers, something we can become vulnerable to is forgetting to make a payment on time. Even if we have the funds in our account, it can be all too easy for it to slip our mind and for us to miss a payment deadline. So what can we do to avoid this happening?

For myself, I am a big fan of setting up direct debits for all of my regular monthly bills. This means my monthly payments were set up automatically when I first opened an account with my internet provider, electricity company etc., and now I do not need to do anything for my bills to be paid on time. Mostly this has worked out well. Except on one occasion where I forgot to cancel the direct debit for the internet after moving out of a flatshare at uni... for over a year! So if you move, or change providers, do make sure to cancel your direct debits.

I understand that not every autistic ADHDer will want to set up automatic payments and that direct debits may not be the best option for you to pay your bills. If that is the case then you can pay them month by month, making individual transactions. However, if you are going to do this, it is important you have a way to remind yourself to pay them on time so that you don't forget. If you need to set something up such as reminders on your phone or another person you can rely on to remind you, please do that!

Missing payments can have a knock-on effect such as more interest being added to what you borrowed (meaning you have to pay back more money than you originally agreed) and your credit score being lowered (which can reduce your options for borrowing money in the future). It can also lead to having more debt than it is manageable for you to pay back.

Another part of managing money as an adult is debt. Debt is when you owe someone money. This can be for several reasons, but the most common ones include taking out a loan to pay for something expensive like a car or to fund university, spending money on a credit card (that you have to pay back at a later date) and using your overdraft (when you spend more money than is in your bank account).

It is likely at some point that we will have some form of debt to pay off during our adult lives, and if we have not been in debt before, the concept of debt can seem very scary! However, taking on debt is not always a bad thing, as sometimes we have to so that we can afford the things we need. As long as the monthly repayments are affordable for us each month, then it will not become an issue in our day-to-day lives. Where debt becomes a problem is when we cannot afford to repay. If you find yourself in a situation where you can't repay I would recommend seeking advice about your options (as I am not a financial expert, I can't provide advice on this). However, when I borrow money and take on debt, there are a few things that I always consider, so that my levels of debt and repayments do not get out of control.

- What is the interest rate?

The interest rate is the amount you pay on top of the amount you originally borrowed. Usually this would be a percentage. For example, if you took a loan of 500 out at a 10% annual interest rate, then you would pay back 550 over the course of a year.

Sometimes you can borrow interest free, meaning you do not pay extra on top. New furniture is one example of something you can sometimes borrow the money for and pay back monthly without paying any additional interest. When it comes to using credit cards, if you pay it off on time, there is no additional interest. But if you don't pay it off on time, then the interest rates can be quite high (which is why you should always be cautious with how much you are spending on a credit card). A fellow autistic ADHDer explained to me why they always try and pay off their credit card before their statement comes in, to avoid the additional interest charges.

> 66 The only thing is if you don't pay within the set amount of time. So I know for me, when my statement comes in on the 6th and then I will have until roughly the 20th to pay that off, otherwise they'll then start charging interest, but for me, I pay it off before my statement even comes in (to avoid interest).

I try to avoid using mine at all costs to avoid credit card debt, and will only use it as a last resort. Interest rates will vary depending on the reason you are borrowing money, and who is lending the money. It is always worth doing comparisons with other lenders as some places will have lower interest rates than others (meaning you will pay back less).

- What are the monthly repayments?

When looking at your options for borrowing money or taking on debt, it is important to know what you are signing up for, and the amount you will need to pay back monthly (and for how long the monthly payments will last). The key is figuring out, along with all your other essential costs, whether you can afford to pay back a certain amount each month. Again you can use tools such as the table earlier to work out how much you can afford to pay back monthly. Sometimes there will be options to have a longer payback period to bring the monthly cost down, so this may be something worth doing if your finances are tight but you still need to borrow money.

- Is it something essential and worth getting into debt for?

The reasons why we may want to borrow money and have debt will vary, but the key thing is making sure we are only borrowing money when we have to. With credit cards, it's very easy to spend money on things we want, but we may not have the ability to pay them back, meaning we end up in more debt than we can manage. For those of us autistic ADHDers who are impulsive, it can be all too easy to spend impulsively on things that are not essential, and this is the reason why I have to be super cautious with myself when using a credit card (because I know that if I am not, I will spend too much on things I do not need). One of the autistic ADHDers I spoke with shared how their use of a credit card, along with physical money generally being used less, had impacted their spending:

> I don't have like a physical concept of money. Yeah, money, is more like it's numbers on my phone. When I have enough numbers, I can use those numbers and get like a new phone or a new watch or a pair of headphones that I want. So it's not... it doesn't seem like it's a big deal when actually, it is because what if something bad happens and then you know, you have to find some money quick.

Unless you absolutely have to, you can decide not to have a

credit card or overdraft option on your account, if you are aware that you may be at risk of impulsive spending unnecessarily. Many people do have credit cards and overdraft options on their bank accounts, but they are not compulsory just because you are now an adult. Also if you do have a credit card, you may be able to lower you credit limit (the amount you are allowed to spend on your credit card) or set payment limits on your bank account. So it may be worth approaching your bank if you feel you are vulnerable to overspending and want to put limits in place to try to avoid any serious consequences from impulse spending.

The ADHD and neurodivergent tax

The 'ADHD tax' describes the additional costs ADHDers have. Some examples of the ADHD tax would include:

- Late fees for missed payments.
- Forgetting to cancel subscriptions we no longer use (or cancel after the free trial is over).
- Forgetting about food we had at home until it is out of date and no longer edible.
- Missing trains or flights, so having to spend extra on a new ticket.
- Forgetting to go food shopping and only realising after the shops are closed, meaning we have to order a takeaway if we want to eat a hot meal in the evening.
- Losing items that cost money to replace.

I have been hit by the ADHD tax far more times throughout my life than I am prepared to admit. The worst incident had to be when I lost my passport while abroad – both the emotional and financial consequences were significant to say the least! Although it is more commonly known as the 'ADHD tax', for myself I see it more as a 'neurodivergent tax', as my autism does also mean I spend more money than if I were neurotypical. For example, I spend more money on things such as bedding than I normally would due to my sensory needs. Also, there have been times I have gotten a taxi due to sensory overwhelm, when public transport was available but I knew that being on a busy train would send me into overload and a potential meltdown. Also we may have safe foods that are the only ones we can eat sensory-wise, and these brands may be more expensive than other similar options.

I suspect that most of us will have additional costs relating to both our autism and ADHD, meaning we experience a double hit from the neurodivergent tax. Again, this is something we may need to consider for our finances, as we may have unexpected costs related to our neurodivergence, and they often do not come with a warning of when they are going to occur!

Some autistic ADHDers may set aside a certain amount each month to cover these unexpected costs when they can. Or, depending on where you live in the world, disabled and neurodivergent people might receive financial support to help cover these additional costs, so it is worth doing your research to see if options are available to you where you live.

Decision making

Now that we have talked about the things many of us autistic ADHDers wish we knew when we were becoming adults, it's time to move onto another important aspect of adulthood: decision making. As you come into adulthood the number of decisions you will need to make will grow, which can be overwhelming at times, but there are tools and questions we can ask ourselves to help. When asking fellow autistic ADHDers about their decision-making approach (in particular for the bigger life decisions), this is what one said:

> Big life decisions that I made myself were always done after a great deal of thought and research – usually months. I'm extremely logical and deliberate in my decision making, and I look at all available evidence and possible outcomes before favouring any options.

For some of us, we may need to take more time to research and consider all facts before making a final decision. We need to go through this process to feel confident in our decisions and that we are making the right choice, which is totally okay! Some people may not understand or may question why we research to the levels we do, but often it is needed due to how our brains work (and how we process information), and we also have to consider our neurodivergent needs when making big life choices.

Although we may realise that we need to put a lot of thought and consideration into our decision making, knowing where to start or how to do this can seem like a daunting task. Especially if you need to make a big choice for the first time. Thankfully, one fellow autistic ADHDer shared their advice on how they have approached making big decisions:

> One is pros and cons lists. Break it down, like, what's the

benefits? What's the negatives? And whichever one wins (or whichever one doesn't seem as bad) is the choice to go with.

Creating a pros and cons list is one way to help us approach big decisions, but they also mentioned the following:

> 66 Another process is just talking it through with people. I find having like a few really close friends who I know that I can just call up whenever and talk it through helps.

Sometimes I do this myself too, when I am fully aware of the options I have, but it is not obvious which one is the best. Talking through my options with somebody I trust (or whose opinion I value) can help to see things from another perspective that I may not have thought about before, and can help me weigh up the pros and cons when there is no clear winning option.

Transitional times in our lives and change can be particularly difficult things to manage for some neurodivergent people, particularly for many autistic people. Especially if we are happy with our situation as children, becoming an adult can be a massive disruption to our lives, and if changes start happening suddenly with no preparation, they can take a massive toll on our mental well-being. So the big question is how can we reduce the risk of this happening?

If we feel we are going to struggle with certain changes, then we can try to take it as slow or as gradual as we need to. Preparing for the changes that come with adulthood as soon as possible is ideal, so we can anticipate any challenges or difficulties and get the right support in place we need during this time and into adulthood as well. Also you may decide to take a break or some time off to manage the changes involved in becoming an adult. For example, some young adults take gap years before starting longer-term commitments such as further education, training or a full time job, and you may want to think about if this is something you want to do also that will help with the transition to adulthood.

One thing I would also like to point out is that not everything will change when we become adults; we will still have our interests and the people who are important to us. So when we do go through big changes during our early adult years, we can still keep many familiar things in our lives the same so we are not overwhelmed with the amount of change all in one go. We can also pace out these changes, and do not have to do them all at once. For example, we could start our first job, but wait a few years before considering if we want to move out of our familiar home or not. I don't think I could have managed all the big mile-stones that are usually part of our early adult years in one go (far too much to take in at once). There are no right or wrong times as to when we make these decisions, and they certainly do not have to all happen the day we turn 18! We can decide when we are ready and the pace of change, and if we need any support. We do not have to follow the timings or expectations of others when it comes to this; the most important thing is that we are in control of when and how these changes happen.

Having considered how much thought can go into making big life choices, along with some strategies to help us make them during your early adulthood, we will now put this into context and look at some of the biggest choices you will likely need to make, such as pursing education further or taking the first steps into the workplace, while also considering your needs and capabilities in relation to your autism and ADHD.

Further education

Although I do see schools and colleges often encourage (and in some cases push) going into higher education and university, it is important to remember that it is your life, and as you come into young adulthood you should have the ultimate choice on how you decide to live it. So if you would rather do something other than more formal education after school, then go for it! But, if higher education or university is right for you, then also go for it! There are a lot of choices and things to consider when deciding to go to university, and support that can be put in place so you are not disadvantaged in comparison to neurotypical students.

Choosing what to study and where are big choices all students have to make before going to university, and sometimes it is not clear which to make first. As it is really important that you enjoy your course, I would say this is what to look for first (if you have flexibility in choosing where you can study). For some, it may be obvious or a natural choice what you will study at university as you have a favourite subject at school or you may want to study a subject that closely relates to your interests. However, if you are still unsure, there are questions that you can ask yourself which can help with deciding what to study:

- What are my strengths?
- What are my strongest subjects at school?

- What career options would I like once I graduate? And which degree subjects open up these options to me?
- Is this subject assessed mainly via coursework or exams? (This will also vary at each university.)
- Will this subject help me get onto a postgraduate course I would like to do in the future? (Either master's or PhD.)

Not every university offers every subject, as there is a wide variety of degrees available that you can study. So if a university does not offer the course you are interested in, you can automatically rule it out. However, there are other things that need to be taken into consideration when deciding which university to study at:

- What are the accommodation options at the university (if living away from home), and do they meet my needs?
- If you are staying at home, what will the commute be like to each university you are considering?
- What is the disability support service like? And can they meet my needs while studying there?
- Does the university offer placement years or work experience options? (If you want to get experience before you graduate.)
- Does the university offer student exchange programmes? (If you want the option to study abroad during your degree.)
- Does the university offer societies and/or sports clubs that I will enjoy?
- Does the university have an autistic or neurodivergent society? (I'm seeing more students set up neurodiversity societies at university, and for some they can be a great form of peer support while studying.)

On both of these lists, some of these questions will be more applicable to you than others depending on your personal goals and circumstances. However, they are a useful starting point if you are trying to decide what you want to study and where. If you are aware that you will need accommodations and adjustments when studying, you may want to prioritise what disability support a university can offer. One of the autistic ADHDers I interviewed opened up about the difficulties they had in accessing accommodations and adjustments while studying:

> I didn't even know about the existence of disability accommodations until college. After I finally got access to them, however, I was disappointed to find out that the people in charge of these services usually have very little experience with neurodivergent people. The process to get accommodations has long, complicated steps, written in complex language, and may require appointments weeks in advance. It's a very hostile process to anyone with challenges in executive function or communication. Then most professors, faculty, counsellors and even doctors don't have personal experience with real ND people, nor training on how to make college more accessible for them. I've found that I usually have to help educate these professionals in what ND brains are really like, instead of the other way around, and it's becoming tiring.

So as you can see, often disability support staff and services just existing within a university or college is not enough. It also depends on how well the staff understand neurodivergence, help put accommodations in place and provide the support needed in relation to communication and executive functioning. So when deciding on where to study, you may want to ask questions around this of disability support departments before committing to a university or college. Also, it is worth factoring in your own neurodivergent needs, such as sensory needs in an educational environment, whether online or face-to-face learning works better for you, or if you'd prefer to study full time or part time.

Employment

Many young autistic ADHDers may find it difficult to figure out what they want to do with their life after school, and that is okay. I spent my late teens and early twenties doing lots of different things until I found a path I actually wanted to go down. However, if you are overwhelmed by your choices, you can seek help from others to help you make an informed choice. For example, if you are considering getting a job then this could be one of your parents or a careers adviser at school, college or university. Some of these people will give you better advice than others, and the key to telling whether they are giving good advice is to ask yourself two questions:

- 'Are they giving me all the information I need so I can make an informed choice?'
- 'Are they trying to persuade me to take a certain path?'

If they are giving you the tools to help explore possible options for the future, then they are helping you to make the right choice for yourself. In contrast, if they are insistent you become an accountant and do not fully consider if this is the right option for you, then they are likely not the best person to be helping you figure out your next steps.

There are often many different factors to consider when looking for a job and deciding on a career, along with additional considerations when you are an autistic ADHDer. These may vary depending on what stage of your life you are at, e.g. if you are just looking for casual work alongside education or if you are looking to start a career. Nonetheless, we will cover aspects that will be relevant for most autistic ADHDers such as disclosure and adjustments, but also how to find a job while considering our neurodivergent needs.

Deciding on the right job

When you are first applying for jobs, along with the normal things you'd consider such as the pay, hours and the main tasks involved with the role, it is also worth considering your own neurodivergent needs in relation to the work on offer. For example, you may know how many hours of work you can manage a week depending on how many spoons you have on a typical week, which will help you decide if you are going to apply for a part time or full time role. Also, something that I have learnt (the hard way) is that your journey to work can also take up a lot of spoons. If this is the case for you, then it would be wise to work out how long a commute you can manage with the number of spoons you have each day. If you do find daily travel too overwhelming, along with working, then it may be an indicator that working from home or locally are the best options.

Of course, sometimes we may be in situations where we may not have much (or any) choice of jobs, and need to take the first thing we can find. Sometimes this may work out, but in the longer term, many autistic ADHDers may find that these jobs are not sustainable. If you are in this situation, it may be a case of accepting a temporary job, while looking for something that is more suited to your neurodivergent needs and considering what will be the right option for you in the longer term.

Disclosure and adjustments

There is always a key question we have to ask ourselves when applying for roles. Do we disclose our autism and ADHD? Or not? There is no straightforward answer to this and it normally depends on various factors and our own personal situation.

For myself, I sometimes disclose on applications, and at other times I do not, depending on the organisation. Given that in recent years I have been working in job roles and organisations related to disability/autism, I felt comfortable disclosing. When disclosing, I do not always say what my disabilities are, I just tick the box saying I am disabled and then list what adjustments I would need during the recruitment process and in the role if I am successful. I do this as I have several disabilities, and it is more efficient to say I am disabled than list them all, and just let them know what my needs are (that is the most important thing for me at least). Employers don't have to know about your disabilities and/or neurodivergence. They also cannot force you to disclose either; it is always your choice how much you tell them about your disabilities, neurodivergence and your related needs.

Note that if you are open online about being an autistic ADHDer, any potential employer might find out by doing a quick Google search on you, even if you do not disclose. Something to be aware of if you are open about being an autistic ADHDer online (nothing wrong with this by the way, I am myself) or in another public forum. It's only once come up for me before when starting a new job, and it was viewed positively (to my relief).

Personally, I find that choosing to disclose or not depends on what I can find out about an organisation through doing my own research, which can sometimes give an indication of whether it will work against me or not if I disclose. However, while some organisations will say things such as 'We are an equal opportunities employer' or 'We welcome disabled applicants', the reality may be different. Sometimes it is a case of organisations wanting to be inclusive but not knowing how to deliver this, or only saying it to portray a certain image. We may not find out if an organisation is ableist until further into the recruitment process, or even until we are working there. So doing prior research into organisations we are applying to can help reduce this risk, but may not eliminate it entirely.

If you are still unsure about if you want to disclose, one way to decide is by considering the following:

- Will I have a fair chance during the recruitment process if I don't disclose?
- Will I face discrimination if I do disclose my neurodivergence?
- Do I need adjustments in the recruitment process to showcase my skills and experiences when applying for roles and/or during the interview?
- Does the employer have a disability employment scheme (or guaranteed interview scheme if you are UK based), or encourage applicants from underrepresented backgrounds?
- If you know anybody who works at the place you are applying for a job, can they give insight into whether it is a good idea to disclose?

- Finding reviews of employers online may inform you of other people's experience of disclosing at an organisation (e.g. Glassdoor or Indeed reviews can be very useful in finding this information out).

The main benefit of disclosing our autism and ADHD is we should have access to adjustments, so that we have a fair chance in the recruitment process and can be successful in the role and maintain it over the long term. So although there is no right or wrong when it comes to disclosing, there are several things to consider when deciding what is the right option.

Recruitment process

Some of you may be familiar with the job application process, but at some point it will have been new for all of us, and this is usually around the same time we become adults. At first, for many people, the process can seem overwhelming, to the point where it is hard to know how to start! Being an autistic ADHDer can make the process of applying for roles more difficult, as there can be a lot of neurotypical norms within applications. However, this does not mean it's impossible. Often we may need to seek advice or support to navigate the process. The more job applications you do over time, the easier it becomes, but when you are doing your first few, there are things to consider that may affect us autistic ADHDers more than other people.

The first step is usually an application form, which often involves filling in answers to many questions online, which I am well aware can be hard when you experience distractibility and other executive functioning challenges. Some autistic ADHDers may need support from another person when filling in an application form, which can vary from having somebody check it over for any mistakes before you press submit, to being supported at each step of filling in the application form. Some autistic ADHDers may find that they can fill in certain parts of the application form no problem, but need help with other parts. If I take myself as an example, I am okay with filling things such as my personal details in myself (as it is usually a case of copy and pasting), but I may need somebody to help me understand any questions being asked as part of the application, and check that my answers make sense too!

For other jobs, you may need to send a cover letter (to show the employer why you want the job and demonstrate you have the relevant skills and a CV/resume). How you write a CV and cover letter will vary depending on the type of job you are applying for and what industry the job is in. To give yourself the best shot at the jobs you are applying for, it is best to research what style of CV/resume is expected for the type of work you are going for. But most CVs/resumes will include your contact details, education, work experience and skills. Also, what is expected on a CV/resume can vary between countries, so if you are new to writing CVs/resumes, make sure you are aware of what needs to be included based on the country you live and are applying for work in.

If you are not sure where to start when it comes to applying for jobs or writing a CV/resume, there are two options you may want to consider. The first is contacting organisations that support neurodivergent people getting into employment. In recent years I have seen either organisations set up specifically to help neurodivergent people find roles or already existing organisations expand to include employment support tailored to the needs of neurodivergent people. They will often provide support for the whole application process, so it is worth seeing if there are organisations close to you (or which operate remotely) that can provide you with this support. The other option is to find on-line resources that provide guidance with writing CVs and cover letters along with templates to help get you started. It is worth making sure you are getting this advice from a credible source if you are looking for advice online, so reputable recruitment and careers websites would be a good place to start. Also, if you are still in education, you may have access to careers advice or a careers department, so do take advantage of this support if you can access it.

Interviews

If an employer likes your application, CV or cover letter, then the next stage of the job application process is usually an interview. The interview will usually involve the potential employer asking questions to see if you have the right skill set for the job, and you will have an opportunity to ask questions too, to see if the job you are applying for is right for you.

Some autistic ADHDers find job interviews difficult, as interviews can involve many neurotypical social norms. The reality is that many people are not fans of the job interview process, but it can be a lot more difficult for many autistic ADHDers, due to the way we process and respond in conversations. For example, many of us need time to consider before responding to complex questions. But in a job interview, we are often put on the spot with lots of complex questions and employers expecting a sleek response without much hesitation. Although some autistic ADHDers may rely on masking to get through a job interview, it can be hard to keep up if we are being bombarded with a million questions without a single second to pause between questions. One autistic ADHDer shared their experiences with interviews and the challenges they faced during a job interview:

> 66 It starts off like I think I have to try to mask, and then I can't for very long and then it slips as we go. I feel a point about midway through where I'm like, Oh no.

There are also unspoken rules within interviews that neurotypicals seem to just know, that for neurodivergent people are not clear by default. The fact that people will often tell 'white lies' (lie about small things) or overexaggerate their actual professional experiences to date to get through a job interview seems to be accepted by many neurotypicals. Whereas autistic ADHDers may communicate honestly about their relevant experience and qualifications, which may not be fully appreciated by interviewers expecting neurotypical responses during an interview. One example is the classic question of 'tell me about your weaknesses':

> 66 Tell me about your weaknesses. And then I tell them about a weakness. And then apparently they don't want to hear a real weakness...

As you can see, if we are 100% transparent with answering this question, we reduce our chances of getting the job. So navigating how to answer questions like this during an interview can be a minefield for autistic ADHDers! During the conversations I had with autistic ADHDers about interviews, some had taken the approach of describing how they overcame a weakness in the past, but this again seemed to be a very hit or miss approach depending on how the interviewer perceived their answers.

So is there anything we can do to help make interviews fair for autistic ADHDers? If I am being honest, most of what needs to change has to come from employers themselves. We can ask for adjustments during the recruitment process, but how accommodating a potential employer may be to this will vary widely. Although I am aware of a select number of organisations that will provide questions in advance (due to processing time) and other accommodations people may need, at the time of writing this seems to be the minority. I have also come across the concept of offering work trials rather than interviews for neurodivergent candidates, but not many organisations have taken this approach (to my knowledge). Offering the right adjustments and alternatives to interviews is the best approach in my opinion, and a cultural shift in the flexibility of the interview process would be ideal. So if any employers and HR professionals are reading this, please take note!

Nonetheless, there are a few things we can do to prepare for job interviews. In many interviews, some of the questions will be the same (or very similar at least), so you can prepare how you'd answer these questions in advance. For example, questions about your previous experience, relevant skills, strengths and areas for development often come up in interviews, so it is worth preparing how you could answer these questions in advance. Also you can practise answering questions in a mock interview before you do the real thing, so that you feel a little more prepared. This could be with somebody you trust in your personal life, or with a careers advisor at your school, college or university. Additionally, if you do decide to contact organisations that specialise in recruitment for neurodivergent people, they should be able to provide support and practise for interviews too.

Your needs at work

Although getting a job is a huge achievement, sometimes this can overshadow our support needs to the point where we start a job and then realise that it is not consistent with our neurodivergent needs. For example, we may only have enough spoons to work part time (along with other commitments we may have) but we take on a full time job, which can lead to burnout very quickly. Something that I did not consider (but wish I had) when I first started working was factoring in the energy levels and executive functioning skills it took to prepare for a day of work in the morning as well as the journey to and from work, on top of working full time! I had taken on more than I could handle, and did not last in the role very long.

For many autistic ADHDers, the sensory environment of work can also have a huge impact on our ability to do the job and maintain our energy levels. We may get a sense of what our working environment will be like during the interview process (as this will usually happen at the place we will end up working), which may be one factor in deciding if we accept the job if offered. Some autistic ADHDers may need adaptations to the environment as part of their adjustments, e.g. noise cancelling headphones or working in a quieter part of the office.

As part of the adjustments process, some people may get an environmental audit of their workplace to help prevent sensory overwhelm at work, so adjustments can be made accordingly (some professionals such as occupational therapists would be able to do this). Examples of what an environmental audit would examine include:

- Visual information:
  - Are there too many visual distractions? Such as certain patterns and shapes.
  - Is the space too cluttered?
  - Are the lights too bright?

- Noise:
  - Are there any background noises that may be distracting?
  - Are there too many people talking in one room (such as an open-plan office), where it may cause an issue?
  - Are there a lot of electrical devices in a working environment, where the noise may become too much for some individuals?

- Space:
  - Is there enough space for movement if required?
  - Are there certain objects or pieces of furniture that could be too easy to bump into (and therefore need to be moved)?
  - Are there any smells that could be overwhelming for some individuals, e.g. certain chemicals if working in a laboratory?

This is by no means an exhaustive list of what an environmental sensory audit may cover, but demonstrates the types of things that may be considered when assessing a working environment. Some employers will be more open to this than others, depending on how inclusive they actually are (rather than how inclusive they claim to be). If an employer is not even welcome to the idea of making these adjustments or having a workplace environment assessed (if you require this), then it may be a red flag or a sign that the employer is not prepared to accommodate your needs relating to your autism and/or ADHD. How long you decide to stay with an employer will always be your choice, but based on other autistic ADHDers' experiences and my own, it may be a struggle to stay long term with employers that won't accommodate your needs.

If sensory processing is a significant factor for you, then it may also be worth using the sensory table from earlier in this chapter (or a similar tool) to help develop a better self-awareness of your own sensory needs, so that you will have a good idea if a certain environment is accessible or will need adjustments to be able to work there.

For other autistic ADHDers, some working environments will be inaccessible, meaning that working there will only cause significant problems in the long term. It is also for this reason that some autistic ADHDers prefer working from home, which can enable people to maintain employment in the long term. On the flip side, though, there are also many autistic ADHDers who cannot work in the same place that they live (and vice versa) meaning that going out of their home to work is essential. It just goes to show the importance of understanding your own needs relating to your autism and ADHD, and making an informed choice – we are not all the same!

Fundamentally, to have the best chance of a job working out in the long term, it is vital that we consider our own needs, capabilities and limitations when it comes to what we can do for work and how much time we can spend working each week. Sometimes it can take a while (and several jobs) to find one where we get this balance right. Based on the conversations I've had with autistic ADHDers, many of us have had difficulties with employment at some point, and this is mainly due to there being some level of imbalance between being able to meet our own needs and managing work simultaneously. As a result, many of us change employers more frequently than most (if we are able to), last in jobs for only short periods of time if we burn out, or our work performance lessens due to burnout and we become at risk of losing our jobs.

Even though I am only in my late twenties at the time of writing, I have probably had more jobs at this point than many people older than me, as I took on roles without considering my needs relating to my autism and ADHD. In my defence I did not discover my autism until I was 23, and 25 for my ADHD, so I was not able to consider these needs properly due to the knowledge I lacked. I more or less suffered in silence before I knew why I was struggling with more typical working routines (e.g. 9–5, five days a week).

There will be times in our lives where we may need to take the first job we can get; most people will experience this at some point (some more often than others). However, if we want to be content with the work we do and be able to sustain it in the long term, then it is essential that we have a strong understanding of our own needs relating to autism and ADHD, and find work or a job that fits in around that and/or an employer who will follow through with making the adjustments we need at work.

Self-employment

For some autistic ADHDers, traditional employment may not be a viable option and the demands from other people while being employed can become too intense, to the point where we would have to compromise our own needs. For this reason, some autistic ADHDers decide self-employment is a better option (or working for themselves).

There are benefits to being self-employed, as you have a lot more choice in how you work, meaning it is a lot easier to fit the work you do around your needs and daily lives. Examples of the benefits include full autonomy on how much work you do, what times of the day you will work and where you complete your work, which can be a lifeline for some autistic ADHDers sustaining employment in the longer term. However, there also comes a lot more personal responsibility – such as managing the finances and taxes of your work (whereas if you were employed, this would likely be done automatically), and you usually have to do a little bit of everything related to your business, rather than one role focusing on your specific skill set.

It is also worth mentioning that you can become self-employed at any point – it is not something you have to do when you first start work. Some people work for another employer first to gain experience and to build up their skills, so that they feel confident in what they are doing when they start to work for themselves. Others may want to work for themselves at the earliest opportunity.

For myself, I have a mix of working for an employer alongside being self-employed, which works well for me. My ADHD seeks variety within the work I do, so I find this combination is the sweet spot for my work. It also means I am no longer job hopping frequently to seek this variety, which has reduced the overwhelm I get from being autistic and having to cope with too many big changes at once. As the income I earn from my self-employed work is variable, I do like the security of knowing that I will be getting a certain amount from my employed work each month to cover my essential bills. It is a very individual choice about if working for yourself or an employer will be the best fit for you, but it took me time to figure out that a combination of employed work and being self-employed was my best option. To be honest, it was only after having the experience of working both for myself and for an employer that I was able to figure this out, so it may be a case of experiencing different ways of working to figure out if being an employee or self-employed (or both) works for you.

Making big decisions about our education or employment as we come into adulthood can be overwhelming; it is likely that these are the first big decisions we will make for ourselves during our lives (rather than our parents or another adult). However, it can also be empowering for us to take ownership of our lives in this way. As one of the autistic ADHDers put it:

66 Being my own advocate and support have made me very determined, because now I know that I understand my own needs better than anybody else; when I do finally make a decision, there's almost no one that can stop me from doing it.

As nobody will understand our needs better than ourselves, we are best placed to make our own choices as adults. Of course, there will be times where we may seek advice from others or need support with our decision making, but ultimately, we decide what is best for us.

4
Relationships and social interaction

Up until this point, I suspect many of us autistic ADHDers would have had our fair share of interactions with our peers during school and growing up in our own communities, which may have been difficult, confusing or not really made much sense to us at all. Although our individual experiences are likely to vary, many of us would have experienced social rejection a lot more than other people, while perhaps not understanding why. For some of us we may have figured out why over time, while for others it may still seem like a complete mystery years later.

However, just as our autism and ADHD do not disappear at 18, neither do the complexities of relationships and social interactions (unfortunately). It's not all bad news though! Many autistic ADHDers do find positive relationships and friendships during adulthood. But some of the difficulties that we experienced growing up can continue into our adult lives. Although there are some similarities to relationships and social interactions to when we were younger (e.g. playground and office politics are often similar once you dig beneath the surface), there are naturally some differences, e.g. romantic relationships, and we will go through them in this chapter. We will start by covering different aspects of social interaction that affect our relationships with a variety of people, such as managing our socialisation levels, masking, maintaining boundaries, impulsiveness and others' responses to our differences. Then in the second part of this chapter, we will take a deeper look into specific types of relationships we will encounter during adulthood, such as friendships, romantic relationships, family dynamics and workplace interactions.

Managing socialisation levels

When it comes to social interaction, there is one important thing to say. There is no obligation to socialise if you do not wish to do so. When we come into adulthood, one thing we have is more autonomy over how to spend our free time. For some autistic ADHDers, that may mean not socialising at all (or only when essential), and if that applies to you, then go for it! There is no point making yourself do something just because it is what others expect us to do. However, some autistic ADHDers like to socialise for some of the time (but still need a lot of time to decompress away from other people), whereas others can be very extroverted and want to spend time with lots of people.

Many autistic ADHDers have some awareness of how much socialising they will want to do, and sometimes the biggest difficulties can be putting into practice the level of socialising we want and/or can manage. For example, an autistic ADHDer may be aware that they only want to socialise for about two to three hours, so to make sure they do not go over this length of time, they may come up with phrases or a plan on how to exit social situations once they've reached their limit, so they don't become stuck on the spot while needing to leave a situation without knowing how to do so. One example of what I've said in the past is that I'm working tomorrow (so I can't stay out late). Often, I found it best to have conversations with people I trust in advance about what I could say when I feel I've reached my social limit, so I can go in prepared with an exit plan if it all becomes too much.

It's also worth noting that the levels of socialisation we want and can manage may change over time. One of the autistic ADHDers I spoke with for the book explained:

> As a teenager and young adult, I found it easier to make friends as I branched out into a more diverse world and found more people like me; however, as I get older, the more I get drained by social interactions. I've become more comfortable with keeping only occasional contact with a few friends, and being alone most of the time. Navigating social interactions is extremely exhausting, even with people I love.

I relate to this experience as well, as there were times in my life where I was more social than I am now. However, in my case I think I underestimated how much socialising I could actually manage, and became burnt out from socialising a lot. I socialise less now to avoid the burnout, which has helped with my personal well-being – I accept the fact that I do not need the same levels of socialising as most other people (which is something I did not realise until I discovered I was neurodivergent in my twenties).

Others may be seeking more social opportunities but are struggling to find them, contributing to feelings of loneliness. Finding out about social groups clubs and events in your local area (and some online communities) is often a good place to start finding new social opportunities. We'll talk about this a little bit more later on when we focus on friendships (including different ways to find new friends).

Masking and appeasing

One of the biggest aspects of trying to get through and in some cases survive social situations for many autistic ADHDers is doing something called masking. You may have come across this term before – ultimately 'masking' (sometimes also called camouflaging) is what people do to blend and fit into social interactions with other people and to hide any outward signs of being neurodivergent. Autistic ADHDers may mask for many reasons, but they're often related to fitting in and blending in socially, so that they appear to be more 'neurotypical'. Some examples of what masking can involve are:

- Copying other people's facial expressions and body language.
- Controlling and overthinking your tone of voice, volume and intonation to blend in socially.
- Suppressing stims and other forms of natural movement.
- Showing enthusiasm for things you cannot stand or find uncomfortable, due to other people's expectations.
- Downplaying your level of interest and/or enthusiasm for topics you truly care about to avoid judgement.
- Feeling pressure to force a smile in social situations (even when it feels unnatural).
- Appeasing people to gain acceptance and to be treated with respect, even if it is at too high a cost to you personally.
- Becoming overly agreeable with people in social interactions

(even if deep down you disagree with what they are saying and/or doing).

- Becoming more quiet, reserved and/or withdrawn than usual due to fear of being fully open with who you are.

For myself, masking started as a response to avoid the pain coming from social exclusion and bullying. The more I masked, the better those around me would treat me, so masking became the only way I could feel slightly safer around my peers. Although I ended up masking to a high level, I never 'passed' as 100% neurotypical, and I was still treated as different (not in a good way) by my peers in school. Still, masking made their responses to me less hostile the closer I seemed to being socially 'normal'. As a result of masking from a young age, I assumed that the only way I would be able to 'earn' people's respect was to appease to others (people please) and ignore all of my needs and wants. As part of my appeasing others, I would use my ability to mask to hide the visible parts of my autistic ADHDer self, as I felt the need to fit in to be respected and dehumanised less.

However, when growing up during my school years, I knew very little about autism and ADHD, let alone masking! There was nobody else at the time who had the ability to counteract my belief that I had to sacrifice so much on a personal level to be treated as a fellow human being. I suspect that many of the autistic ADHDers reading this have had similar experiences, so if that is the case for you, then I will be that person now: know that we all deserve to be treated with respect as humans, and it is not okay for us to be treated as less than due to being autistic ADHDers. If we can, we should have as little contact (and ideally none at all) with people who make us feel we have to change our whole selves for them to see us as human too.

For many autistic ADHDers being in social environments where we have no choice but to mask a lot of the time, masking itself can become less of a conscious thing we do in specific situations, to becoming our default way of being around other people, as if we are on auto pilot. For me, this meant that the only times I wasn't masking was when I was home alone with my fur babies!

Masking often takes a lot of effort and if we mask a lot of the time, this can have a significant impact on our well-being and health. Ideally, autistic ADHDers would live in a world where we would not need to mask at all. Unfortunately, appearing to be different in our society still often comes with stigma, harassment, bullying and in some cases threats to our personal safety, particularly if we experience additional forms of marginalisation besides being neurodivergent. This is why wider societal change is needed so we no longer need to mask our autism and ADHD, and all autistic ADHDers can unmask without fear of negative consequences. Although organisations and neurotypical people are starting to acknowledge neurodiversity and autism acceptance has been growing in more recent years, there is still a way to go. It is one of many reasons why some autistic ADHDers become activists and advocates for change within our communities, as we do not want other autistic ADHDers to have to mask to the levels that many of us have had to for safety while simply trying to exist and live as our real selves.

The reason why many autistic ADHDers feel strongly about pushing back on this is because of the mental health consequences of masking, which often leads to significant burnout, low mood and anxiety. 'Keeping up appearances' makes us unwell. Some of us will mask intensely for years, if not decades, as a form of survival in neurotypical social spaces. In the short term, masking will help us 'get through' social interactions, meaning we appear to be having 'successful' social interactions (or what is seen as successful by neurotypical standards), and so we start to mask more frequently. However, for many of us, this will lead to masking automatically when socialising, and all too often the mental effort required to mask in all of our social interactions (even if it is automatic) will have a negative impact on our personal well-being in the longer term. Also, depending on our circumstances, any kind of unmasking could be potentially dangerous for our personal safety. So although ripping off the mask straight away can feel like the most desirable thing to do when we come to realise the impact masking has on a personal level, some of us may need to consider potential risks before we unmask and we may need to think about how and where we can unmask safely first. For some autistic ADHDers, finding other neurodivergent people and friends can lead to being in spaces where it is safer to unmask (and there is less social pressure to conform), or they might start to unmask around the people closest to them. For other autistic ADHDers, simply having alone time or engaging in our hobbies is the best way for us to unmask and be our true selves. One of the autistic ADHDers I interviewed also shared the importance of finding places and people where they could be their authentic self:

> Finding people and environments where I'll be accepted as I am is the most important thing to me now. I've stopped expecting support from places that I know I won't get it (like my family or the community where I grew up) and instead prioritise finding friends I can be open with.

Unmasking is often a slow process, and takes a conscious effort, due to many of us masking as an automatic response for many years. If/when you decide to unmask, it is often easiest to start with something small and gradually build up to fully unmasking, as we often learn more about our authentic selves as we unmask away from the pressures of social norms. For me, one example of unmasking was saying no to social events I did not have the energy for. Whereas previously I would have felt pressure to say yes, or I would have come up with some elaborate excuse as to why I couldn't make it. And when I was fully masking, I was aware that I couldn't make up excuses too often, otherwise people would start to realise something was up or think something was wrong with me. If we do unmask, this may also impact our current relationships, as people only know the masked version of us, and may be surprised to see us 'change'. Depending on the person this could be a positive or a negative experience, so I will admit it will always be a bit of a gamble if we unmask; the knock-on effects it may have on our relationships are unknown.

My social circle became a lot smaller when I started to unmask around people I trusted when discovering I am an autistic ADH-Der. Some of those people are still a part of my life, but others are not, as we only got on well when I was masking. Although it was difficult to deal with at the time, it has turned out for the better, as I now know who exactly I can be my real self around while continuing to have good relationships with them. Unmasking is still an ongoing process for me, despite it being several years since I started trying to mask less. I only feel safe to unmask in certain situations or around certain people, so it would require a massive cultural shift for me personally to unmask 24/7 every-where (hence why some of us campaign and advocate for ac-ceptance and changes in society). However, in the places where I feel safe to unmask, it has taken away a lot of the pressure and self-criticism, and I am happier for it.

Boundaries

Another aspect that comes along with the different types of relationships we have is boundaries. Boundaries when it comes to relationships (and our social interactions) are limits people put in place so that they feel comfortable in their relationships. Boundaries in our relationships can range from how much time you are spending interacting with a person to whether you feel comfortable giving a hug. Boundaries within relationships is something that is not often talked about, and as a result many people will assume that we have the same boundaries as them, which isn't helpful and can be difficult to navigate. Below are a list of common boundaries that people may have:

- **Emotional boundaries** – How much you feel comfortable sharing and expressing your emotional state with the people around you.
- **Physical boundaries** – How much personal space you may need and how you feel about others physically touching you.
- **Sexual boundaries** – What you feel comfortable doing sexually with another person.
- **Mental boundaries** – What you feel and do not feel comfortable discussing with other people.
- **Material boundaries** – How you feel about others borrowing or using your personal possessions.
- **Spiritual boundaries** – Boundaries that come from your religion and/or personal beliefs.
- **Time-related boundaries** – How much time you want to spend doing certain activities or interacting with other people.

The assumptions that many people make around personal

boundaries can cause several difficulties for many of us autistic ADHDers. Firstly, as we experience the world in different ways (particularly sensory wise), what most other people see as fine may cause problems that can be difficult for us to tolerate, especially with our differences with sensory processing. A common one (that I'm sure many of us have experienced at some point) is being expected to hug a relative who squeezes us too tightly while being overwhelmed with the smell of the fragrance they are wearing. Secondly, as many people won't explicitly say what their boundaries are (and we do not automatically make the same or similar assumptions as neurotypicals), this can often lead to us unintentionally crossing somebody else's boundaries. For example, we may be talking in depth about our interests and not realise straight away when the person we are talking to wants to leave the conversation.

When it comes to stereotypes associated with ADHD and autism, I can think of many examples of how we are portrayed as always crossing neurotypical people's boundaries, but not the other way round. However, in reality neurotypical people frequently cross our boundaries without realising too. Many autistic ADHDers feel unable to raise issues related to others crossing our boundaries due to our need to mask in many social interactions. Also, many autistic ADHDers have likely had negative experiences in the past when trying to advocate for our needs, due to a lack of understanding from others. In many ways, autistic ADHDers often have to ignore their own boundaries and needs to get by day to day. In addition, autistic ADHDers often have to be hyperaware of potential boundaries that neurotypical people have, as if we cross them without realising, the consequences are more likely to be bigger, due to us being in the social minority and others being unable to understand our perspective.

So in my view, the stereotype is very misleading, and does not consider how much emotional energy autistic ADHDers often need to put in when it comes to boundaries. Issues relating to boundaries tend to arise due to our differences from other neurotypes, rather than autistic ADHDers deliberately trying to cross them. So please do not take on the full blame if something goes wrong related to others' boundaries (easier said than done I know, especially if the blame has been directed at you due to your autism and/or ADHD). Communication is always a two-way street, so when boundaries-related issues arise it is likely that a misunderstanding has taken place on both sides.

Nonetheless, if we do make a mistake and cross a boundary, it is important we acknowledge what went wrong, take responsibility (if needed) and have a conversation with the person whose boundary we crossed, to avoid repeating the same mistake. In some cases, the other person may not be open to having a conversation. So in this situation we need to respect their decision and not push it any further with them. For some autistic ADHDers, this can be difficult, especially if there is some confusion about the situation that occurred. Talking about what happened with a trusted person can be helpful for some, whereas others may feel taking a self-reflective approach is more useful for them. Also, if you have access to a therapist or counsellor then you could also discuss any misunderstandings of boundaries with them too.

As a result of negative social experiences many autistic ADHDers have experienced, and/or our neurodivergent-related needs, we may feel the need to create strong boundaries over time. One of the autistic ADHDers I interviewed opened up about how their social experiences meant that they:

" felt and built up my boundaries like a wall of bricks. Whereas once upon a time I exposed myself to vulnerable situations and I didn't really know how to get out of them.

Boundaries are often important to create, in order for us to be and feel safe. Our boundaries will be unique to us and will usually be based on our past interactions and experiences. However, if we have not practised putting boundaries in place before, it can be hard to know where to start, and if you are not sure, we will now look at ways we can set our own boundaries.

How to set our boundaries

The first step of setting boundaries is to recognise what boundaries we already have. Some autistic ADHDers may already have a clear idea of what these are. Others may be unsure. Figuring out what your own boundaries are isn't always the easiest of tasks and it can take some time before we have a clear understanding of our boundaries. As the boundaries we do have are unique to us, following a prescribed step-by-step guide to 'figuring out our boundaries' is likely not the best way to approach this. However, there are questions we can ask ourselves that can help us start the process of identifying what boundaries we may have. Some examples include:

- Are there any particular topics in conversations that usually make me feel triggered, stressed or uncomfortable?
- Are there any activities that I feel pressured into doing, that I can't stand or feel uncomfortable participating in?
- Do I feel the need to be guarded during certain social situations?

- Are certain activities taking up too much of my time, or using too many of my spoons (i.e. my energy)?
- Do I feel uncomfortable with how somebody is physically touching me (this could be anything from somebody standing too close for comfort, to a light hug or sexual contact).
- Are people using/touching my personal possessions in a way I do not like? Or which makes me feel uneasy?
- Does what other people are saying and/or doing around me go against my personal beliefs and values?

Once you have identified your boundaries, the next step will be practising putting them in place. Establishing boundaries in real-life situations can seem incredibly daunting and can be stressful due to the uncertainty of how others may respond when stating our needs. If we have identified a number of boundaries that need to be put in place, doing it all at once can seem overwhelming and can become more stressful than not having the boundaries established at all. So when you start using your boundaries in daily life it can often be easier to start small, putting in place just one or two boundaries and building from there at a pace that feels right. Depending on where you are at emotionally, you may need to establish boundaries more quickly than this approach, which is okay. Gradually putting boundaries in place is often a preferred approach for those who have anxieties about establishing boundaries or for people who are just getting started.

Some autistic ADHDers may know what boundary they want to put in place but it can be difficult to know what words to use in a conversation to achieve this. If this is the case, it may be worth planning and practising what you are going to say. This is something I have personally found hard over the years, but it has been helpful to draft one or two sentences of how I can comfortably (or as close to comfortably) state what my boundary is, and then ask somebody I trust for their opinion on how I am asserting my boundary. When I was lacking confidence in how I planned to communicate my boundaries to others, getting a trusted second opinion helped put me at ease and follow through with establishing the boundary.

There are no exact right or wrong ways to establish a boundary. However, if you are not sure where to start or how to plan establishing a boundary, some of the following phrases may be helpful (or at least a starting point):

- I feel _____ when people talk about _____/say _____ to me.
- When _____ happens, this makes me feel _____.
- Thank you for inviting me, but I need to check if I can make it before saying yes or no.
- I would love to, but I am really busy and don't have enough spare time right now.
- Thank you, but I am not interested/do not feel comfortable with doing this.

The phrases above can be adapted depending on the boundary you are setting and can be changed to sound more like you in everyday conversations, but hopefully this will give you some idea of how you could communicate boundaries if this is something that does not come naturally to you. Putting boundaries in place is something that often takes practice and time before people feel comfortable with doing it. So if things don't go exactly to plan when you start putting boundaries in place, that is okay and you won't be the only person who feels this way (far from it). Sometimes you may need to take a step back to reflect, talk through what happened with someone (if you find that helpful) and try again at setting boundaries when you feel ready.

Asserting your boundaries can also be difficult as sometimes people feel guilty about it. Guilt that comes from establishing boundaries can be due to a variety of reasons, but one I've noticed is fairly common among autistic ADHDers is previous experiences of people not understanding their boundaries (relating to their neurodivergence) and consequently being dismissive. If a person is continuingly being dismissive and unwilling to respect your boundaries, it's not a good sign for building a strong friendship or relationship in the long term. This can be particularly hard if these people are family members or people we live with who will in some way be present in our lives; this can add to our guilt. How you decide to navigate boundaries in these situations is likely going to be unique depending on your personal situation, so don't feel you have to follow others' advice exactly if they do not understand your situation.

People's responses to our neurodivergence

If you have known about your autism and/or ADHD for a while, you will have likely already experienced other people's responses when they find out about your neurodivergence. If you discovered you are an autistic ADHDer later on, then figuring out how people may respond if you decide to disclose your neurodivergence can be tricky. There are many potential responses that people may have, but some of the more common ones include:

- People thinking they understand because their family member/friend/somebody they know is an autistic ADHDer, but they may not understand our needs as individuals.
- People who are dismissive and/or have out-of-date views about autism and ADHD.
- People who genuinely want to understand and are prepared to listen/help.
- Some who are not interested in what we have just said to them.

Some of these responses sadly reflect the stigma, bias and lack of understanding around autism and ADHD in our society. If somebody's response to your disclosure is hostile or dismissive, then you absolutely do not have to engage with that person further and put up with what they're saying or doing towards you. Over the years, I've learnt it's not worthwhile to appease people who show no willingness to understand, and that I'm far better off not interacting with them. Although some autistic ADHDers may be tempted to try and educate, it's not our responsibility to do so (it's theirs!). Obviously, I am talking about worst-case scenarios here and I hope this is something you've never experienced yourself. It's highly unlikely that this will happen every time you disclose, but there's always some level of risk when mentioning our differences, particularly to people we don't know well.

It's important to remember that it's always your decision if you do decide to tell other people, and that if you are worried about the responses of others, you do not have to let them know about your autism and ADHD. Often, it's about weighing up your personal pros and cons in certain social situations to see if it's in your best interest to mention your neurodivergence. Even if we choose not to mention autism and ADHD, other people still may notice differences with our social interactions and could make assumptions and judgements about them. Regardless of how long I've been aware of my autism and ADHD, it's likely at some point somebody picked up on some differences. Some people may not comment, and others will.

Impulsiveness and social interaction

It's also worth bearing in mind how some of our impulsiveness can also impact our social interactions. Many of us will speak our thoughts as soon as they arise. This isn't necessarily a bad thing; it can lead to really engaging conversations. However, it can also mean we say things before fully thinking through the impact words may have or their consequences. When it comes to social relationships, people may make incorrect assumptions about our intentions or take what we say the wrong way, which can create difficulties in establishing and maintaining friendships, particularly in the early stages.

When this happens, some people may choose to disclose their autism, ADHD or both, whereas some people may just explain that they have a tendency to speak out loud to process their current thoughts. This approach can help when social interactions get awkward or with small misunderstandings. Again you don't have to explain why – it's your choice how much you tell other people. You do not have to say anything at all as to the reasons why you may be communicating differently from societal expectations. As no two social interactions are the same, sometimes it is easier to decide on the best approach to take based on the situation and who you are interacting with. Also, how other people respond may impact on what you choose to do in these situations. We are not responsible for other people's reactions, and if things do not go well (or there is a lack of understanding/willingness to understand) then it is often a sign that the friendship is not a strong one.

However, it is important to note that having impulsive tendencies does not mean we have a 'get out of jail free' card to avoid accountability if we cause harm or offence when speaking impulsively. If our impulsiveness leads to us saying something that does cause harm and/or offence it's important that we take responsibility for it, try to make amends and take the time to reflect on what steps need to be taken to avoid the situation from happening again. Anyone has the potential to cause harm and offence, even if it wasn't their intention, and autistic ADHDers are not exempt from this.

An example of when my impulsiveness caused offence was during my teen years when I told one of my relatives that they 'looked three months pregnant' because they were wearing a swimsuit that was a bit too tight for them (without realising I should have taken some time to pause and think of a better way to respond). This is something I wouldn't dream of saying now, but they asked for my opinion, and I didn't realise that being 100% honest with the first thought that came into my mind would lead to a falling out.

So what can we do to minimise harm or offence through being impulsive? One example is if you have even the slightest bit of doubt about what you are going to say in the moment and its impact, it may be worth speaking with someone you trust to get a second opinion on your impulsive thoughts before sharing them with everyone. However, if there isn't somebody there who you can speak with, it may be worth noting them down in private and taking the time to consider their potential impact if said out loud. Everyone has likely had at least one moment in their life where they have said the wrong thing during a social interaction (anybody who claims otherwise is probably lying). The key thing in these situations is learning from them so we do not repeat the same mistakes.

Let's take the example above, telling one of my relatives that they looked three months pregnant. If that specific thought came into my head, I would make a 'hmmmm' noise at first. There are several benefits of doing this: it gives me a few seconds to think of a better response (that still reflects my true thoughts); satisfies my impulse to say something/use my vocal cords instantly; and also gives the impression that I am mentally still present in the conversation. I would then say something along the lines of 'Are you comfy in the swimsuit? I like the colour but I wouldn't want you to be too uncomfortable if it feels tight'. Again, this is just one potential way to approach the situation. As I was asked for my opinion on the spot, I did not have the time to check with somebody I trusted for their thoughts on how to answer this question. Taking a longer pause before responding would be the most comfortable way for me to handle this situation if it happened today.

Friendships and double empathy

Friendships are usually formed when we share a mutual connection with someone and enjoy spending time with each other. Often friendships can develop from a place of shared interests or having similar qualities and values. Some autistic ADHDers will have had friendships during childhood and some of these friendships may have lasted just a short period of time, whereas others may have been stronger and lasted over the long term. Throughout both childhood and adulthood, I have had plenty of short-term friends, where once we got to know each other a bit better it became obvious the friendship was not going to work out. And I have had a few friendships that have developed slowly and have lasted over the long term.

I think the biggest challenge for autistic ADHDers is the differences most of us have in our natural way of communicating. These differences in social communication, and the challenges they can bring, are described in the 'double empathy problem'. The double empathy problem was proposed by autistic academic Damion Milton (2012), in which he argues that autistic and non-autistic people often experience difficulties in making social connections due to each person not understanding the other's communication style. So it's both the non-autistic person not understanding the autistic person, and the autistic person not understanding the non-autistic person. Although this theory is a generalisation, it can be helpful in understanding why potential friendships did not work out, and why socialising can feel more difficult or challenging than for most other people.

There are many autistic ADHDers who recognise this and seek out friendships with other autistic ADHDers/neurodivergent people, as it can be easier to form a social connection with people who have a similar communication style. I will say though that just because somebody else is an autistic ADHDer or neurodivergent does not mean you will automatically form a friendship, but it may be easier to start one or find a mutual connection compared to with neurotypical people. Two fellow autistic ADH-Ders recognised something similar when reflecting back on their childhood experiences and who they ended up hanging out with, both in groups and on a one-to-one basis:

66 As a child, I identified as a 'weird kid', and when I got bullied, found solace in hanging out with the other 'weird kids'. But many of us were ND, too, which we only realised when we got older. Maybe I'm just a 'weird kid' AND neurodivergent as hell.

66 One of my best friends, he's both autistic and ADHD. He couldn't get on with anybody else. But I can and we're great friends. It just sort of seemed like of all the people, he would gravitate towards me, and I now know it's because I am neurodivergent but growing up, I didn't know why.

After discovering my own neurodivergence in early adulthood, I started to interact with the neurodivergent people (both online and in person), and although I have formed some very strong friendships, not every interaction has developed into a friendship. Sometimes we can have clashing traits and conflicting needs with fellow autistic ADHDers, meaning there can be barriers in forming friendships and relationships.

If you have experienced this before with other neurodivergent people, it can be all too easy to be hard on yourself emotionally, especially if you have experienced a lot of social rejection over the years. It is okay if we do not gel with another neurodivergent person or if our needs clash, there's no rule that dictates that we all have to be best friends! Sometimes it is best to acknowledge when a friendship is not going to develop rather than forcing it just because we share a similar or the same neurotype.

However, from speaking with other autistic ADHDers (and from my own experiences) one of the most common challenges comes with forming friendships with neurotypical people. This is often because neurotypical people are usually a lot more subtle with their social cues, which can make it harder to interpret for those of us with a different communication style. For example, a neurotypical person may start looking away if they are disengaging from a conversation, whereas for many of us, looking away is the only way we can focus on what another person is saying and engage.

The way we relate to others can often be different to neurotypical people, which can cause difficulties when trying to form friendships. One autistic ADHDer I spoke with shared how their expression of empathy is generally better understood by other neurodivergent people:

66 A neurodivergent person isn't (usually) turned off by you telling your stories. Many neurodivergent people see that you are just trying to give an example of how you can empathise with a situation that they've been through too.

From my discussions with fellow autistic ADHDers, it seems many of us tell our own stories of similar situations to relate to other people and to empathise. However, if we are interacting with a neurotypical person, it can often not be perceived that way, with some making the assumption that we are centring ourselves when they are suffering, when more often than not, we are actually trying to show we understand the pain they are experiencing.

Unfortunately many neurotypical people have little understanding of autism, ADHD and neurodiversity more generally, meaning that their biases can have a negative impact on us when seeking to form friendships and make social connections. A fellow autistic ADHDer reflected on their experience of this bias, before they were aware of their neurodivergence:

66 Sometimes people don't take a liking to you, and not knowing why, and now thinking it's probably just because they can sense I was autistic.

So even though nobody involved with this interaction (at the time) knew they were autistic, their differences were picked up on, leading to negative assumptions and responses from the other person. Again, people who respond in this way will not be our friends, and it is best to not interact with those (if possible) who discriminate against us for not being neurotypical.

Another aspect of friendship that many autistic ADHDers can experience is not initially recognising the difference between friendships and acquaintances. Many autistic ADHDers consider every person they have regular positive and neutral interactions with as a friend (no matter how frequently they interact). Whereas many neurotypical people will view the people who they have brief and friendly interactions with differently to their friends, as they consider friends to be people who they have a deeper personal connection with and spend a lot more time with doing activities together. Sometimes a challenge that can arise from this is when we are interacting with people who may have a different perspective on who is a friend compared to an acquaintance. One person may feel they have a close friendship with somebody, but the other person may see them as just an acquaintance. Also sometimes people may be friendly and claim to be friends during conversations, but do not seek out meaningful interactions with us; this is often a sign of them being an acquaintance rather than a true friend. Additionally, as you get to spend more time with somebody, it can be hard to tell if a friendship is developing or not, especially if the communication style of the person we are interacting with is significantly different to ours, or is not clear to us.

So when we are in a situation where we are not sure if somebody is a true friend or not, we can have mixed feelings and doubts about where we stand with them, which can have a knock-on effect on our social confidence. For some autistic ADHDers, figuring out if somebody is a genuine friend or just somebody who is nice to us can be a helpful step. As part of this process it may be worth asking yourself the following:

- Am I the person who always initiates (or starts) our conversations? Or does it vary between both of us? If you are almost always starting the conversation, then it could be a sign that they are not prioritising developing the friendship.
- Are conversations with this person mainly small talk (e.g. mainly talking about generic topics such as the weather or traffic)? Or do they ask meaningful questions about my life and interests? Do they enjoy sharing jokes and/or memes with me? If most conversations you have are strictly small talk, then they are more likely to view you as an acquaintance.

This is by no means how all autistic ADHDers view their friendships and relationships, but autistic ADHDers viewing acquaintances and friendships similarly (if not the same) has come up many times when interacting with autistic ADHDers, so I thought it was worth mentioning.

Additionally, for autistic ADHDers who learn and process information visually, diagrams such as the one below can be helpful if we want to gain a better understanding of how close we are with different people in our lives, if it is not clear. I have created one example of a relationship circle below. However, depending on our cultures and individual circumstances, our own relationship circles will look different, e.g. some people may be closer with their friends rather than their family members. No two autistic ADHDers' relationship circles will look exactly the same!

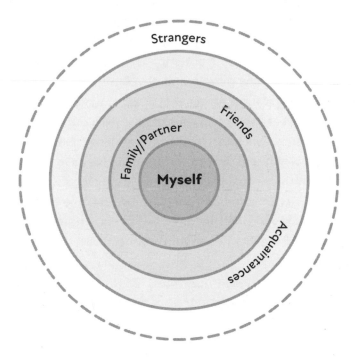

When seeking friendship, it can be tricky to figure out where to start or even where to meet people to make friends. When we are younger, social events and interactions are usually planned or organised by the adults in our lives. As adults, it can be less clear where to seek out these interactions. Many young people (including neurotypicals) find it harder to meet new people as their responsibilities increase and their free time decreases.

However, there are still opportunities and places we can go to meet people and find potential new friends. One good place to start is to see if there are any clubs or societies based around your interests in your local area. Often a Google search or searching on websites such as Meetup can be a good place to start. Also, there are communities and social groups online where there are opportunities to meet new people, but it is important to remain vigilant when interacting online, as there can be additional risks with internet safety. Some autistic ADHDers during adulthood are able to meet new people and develop friendships through their work or education. As many of us are at work or studying for most of our week, we spend a lot of time with our colleagues or fellow students, which can lead to developing friendships if we get on well with them. This does not mean we have to be close friends with the people we work or study with, as we are likely to get along with some people at the workplace better than others. I will say having friends at work tends to make it more enjoyable if we are lucky enough to connect with the people we interact with daily.

Another aspect of friendship that autistic ADHDers need to be mindful of is when friendships turn sour, and what the red flags are that a friendship we thought was real is actually superficial when we dig beneath the surface. One key sign of whether a friendship is genuine is how much you put on a social mask around the person you consider your friend.

After discovering I am an autistic ADHDer, at first I thought it would be safe to 'unmask' around people I considered close friends. Although some of those people I initially unmasked around are still friends today, some are certainly not. I was actually shocked by how quickly some friendships ended as soon as I unmasked, even if it was only a little bit of unmasking. Reflecting back now, something that is clear was that many of my friendships were built upon my social performance of 'acting normal' by neurotypical standards, and when I started to show my authentic self, it made me realise that a fair few of the friendships I had were not compatible with my authentic self and only the masked version of myself. Although it stung at the time on a personal level, I am happier now, as my friendships are based on who I truly am and it removes the pressure to mask when it is just us.

Another sign that a friendship may not be genuine is if somebody is coming to us for a favour or is using us in some way, and are not interested in other aspects that normally come with friendships, such as a shared connection, wanting to see how we are feeling or wanting to do activities together. Most friends usually do each other favours occasionally when needed; this should be a two-way street if it is a genuine friendship and not one-sided. If somebody who seems like a friend always wants something from you, and would not help you in return, this is often a red flag, and they are likely trying to take advantage.

Similarly, if you are struggling, going through a hard time or need support, and this person who seems like a friend is not prepared to help in any way (or at least help you to access the right support if they cannot provide it themselves), then they are likely not a true friend. Even if they act friendly towards us when they are seeking something, this will likely be for their own gain, as real friendships are a two-way street.

Friendships can also be both one-to-one on an individual level, or part of a wider friendship group. Autistic ADHDers can experience challenges with navigating friendship groups, which can be quite different from one-to-one interactions. One autistic ADHDer who contributed towards this book gave some insight into trying to navigate social and friendship groups:

> 66 When I got to high school, I would bounce between the different groups. I kind of fit in with the edgy gamers and then would kind of fit in with the nerdy people that would be in the library. And then I'll kind of fit in with some of the anime people even though I don't like anime and it was just like I would just bounce between different groups. But I never felt like I fitted in. Which is quite tricky, but when it comes to friendships, it's more like I've never liked groups. I've always liked sort of one-on-one friendships.

I relate to this, as I have lost count over the years of the times I have tried to fit into a friendship group, but I always felt like I was on the outskirts. I would be part of the conversation but struggled to know the exact moment to contribute. I found the pauses where people would know when to start speaking were a nanosecond long and too quick for me to pick up on until it was too late. Or I would think of how I was going to respond, but by the time I thought of what to say, the group conversation had already moved on to another topic.

There were some friendship groups that were easier to navigate than others. This was mainly because I had made friends with some of the people in the friendship group individually first, which made it a smoother transition into becoming a member of the friendship group over time. It felt like a more natural way to be part of a friendship group, rather than being on the edges trying (and often failing) to jump in when possible. However, even in these situations where I became a part of a friendship group more authentically, I could still sense that not everybody in the group wanted me to be there, let alone form any kind of friendship. I did not understand at the time, but now I know I'm an autistic ADHDer, it is obvious that they did not like me due to how my neurodivergence presented (despite masking), and some ended up having a rather hostile attitude towards me when I was part of the group. So even in situations where I got on with most of the people in a group, there was rarely an absence of ableism and bullying growing up.

Because of these experiences during my school days, for a while I stayed away from friendship groups and preferred to interact with people one on one. This was usually a safer way to socialise and took up fewer of my spoons! As some time has passed since my school days, I've found that I have started to interact in friendships groups again, but these are mainly made up of other neurodivergent people, which was rarely the case before. I do, however, still have a preference for socialising with others in smaller groups or one on one, due to how much socialising I can manage and to reduce the risk of being with people who are hostile. How you decide to socialise and form friendships (whether part of a group or one to one) is always up to you. However, it may be worth considering your own needs related to friendship, as these may differ from others and affect how you socialise.

As you can see, friendships are often complex and it can feel like a minefield at times trying to figure out who is a friend and who is not. Often this can take time, and friendships rarely develop overnight. Often it is a case of trial and error until you find the right people to develop friendships with. Unfortunately, there is no magic formula for social interactions or building friendships (otherwise I'd be writing it here for you and this part of the book would be a lot shorter!), but once you find the people you connect with, friendships should be a source of happiness and enjoyment that adds value to your life and creates wonderful memories.

Romantic relationships

66 I figured if I kept mingling with my friends in school, a great relationship would eventually come along. And it did.

When we come into our early adulthood, one of the new types of relationships some of us may have are romantic. Despite what societal pressure says, you do not have to engage in romantic relationships if you don't want to; the choice is entirely yours. Some autistic ADHDers may also be aromantic or asexual, which will affect how they engage with romantic relationships, if they choose to do so at all. However, for autistic ADHDers who want to engage in romantic relationships, there can be some additional things to navigate and consider, which we will go through now. I should point out though that this section of the book is by no means a comprehensive guide to finding a partner or the 'one', but rather it covers how our autism and ADHD can interplay with our romantic experiences.

One of the most difficult things in the area of romantic relationships is at the beginning: trying to figure out if the other person is interested. Especially as people who are different neurotypes from ourselves may not communicate their interest directly or in a way that is clear to us. For example, somebody may be flirting with us but it may be very subtle and we may interpret it as them being friendly towards us. This can also work the other way around, where we may interpret someone's friendliness as romantic interest (confusing I know). If I'm being honest, I have experienced both sides of the coin when it comes to this, which has led to some awkward situations!

So the big question is how to figure out if the other person is interested? Although everyone will have their own way of indicating interest, some clues a person may give are: complimenting you (more so than a friend), seeking to spend more time with you, finding shared interests and activities to do together, asking lots of questions and being interested in getting to know you better. Others may use their body language or facial expressions to communicate they are interested, which may not be as easy to pick up on. Some examples of how people use body language or facial expressions to show romantic interest include looking towards you (more than others would), or if their body language changes when talking to you compared to others, e.g. they may stand taller when you are around, or they may blush and smile when interacting with you. Many people will show their interest through a combination of their actions, body language and facial expressions, while some may show their interest in you through one of these factors more than the others, depending on their own natural communication style.

If you are still uncertain and feel the need to seek clarity, one option is to ask directly. Depending on the person you're interacting with, this could be really hit or miss and some people may struggle with direct communication, whereas others will appreciate your honesty. Something that I've come to realise over the years is that things are more likely to go smoothly if both of us can understand each other's communication style with relative ease. This doesn't mean we have to communicate exactly in the same way (it's unlikely that humans will ever communicate in identical ways), but if we can understand each other and our communication with each other feels natural most of the time, this is usually a positive sign.

Something that can be nerve racking is making the first move. Being nervous about this interaction is certainly not unique to autistic ADHDers, but can be more challenging to navigate, especially if we experience rejection sensitivity (discussed more in the following chapter), previous experiences where it has gone wrong or both.

People often make the first move by flirting. Although some autistic ADHDers appreciate and enjoy flirting, there are many who do not, as flirting is often heavily reliant on neurotypical communication. Ultimately for those of us who don't like flirting, or do not pick up on it automatically, it can be challenging knowing the best way to let somebody know how we feel. As I mentioned before, speaking directly about how we feel is an option. If you do decide to be direct early on, be aware that some people may find this overwhelming, while others will prefer the honesty. You'll never really know if saying directly how you feel will work, so it is a bit of a risk, but it may pay off! Even if you do not get the response you're hoping for when making the first move, it is always vital to respect the other person's viewpoint and not to push things further.

This leads on nicely to a vital part of romantic relationships: consent. Consent means that everybody involved is happy to take part and has agreed to do something together. This can involve anything from holding hands, to kissing, to sex (and everything in between). It's always vital that consent is given, as significant harm can be caused to someone who has not consented, and it is also a criminal offence to engage in sexual activity without consent. How you communicate consent and not consenting is a conversation you need to have with your partner. How consent is given (or not) will vary between couples and people. However, many autistic ADHDers process social communication literally, so directly saying 'yes' or 'no' may be needed to ensure everyone involved understands whether consent has been given.

However, there are people out there who prefer to indicate consent in a more subtle way that some autistic ADHDers may find it difficult to pick up on, leading to ambiguity over whether consent has been given. If you're ever unsure if somebody has given consent or is asking for your consent, you should always ask as it's better to be safe than sorry, due to the potential consequences.

When it comes to romantic and sexual relationships, one key element that will be applicable for autistic ADHDers is our partners understanding our differences (unless of course our partner is also an autistic ADHDer or a similar neurotype to us). Obviously, how much you reveal to a partner (and when) about you and your divergence will always be your choice. However, if you are forming an intimate relationship with somebody, they will likely notice some of our difference over time, and there may be occasions where we need to explain some things that they may not understand if they do not know we are autistic ADHDers or neurodivergent.

The response we may get when telling a partner about our autism and/or ADHD could be positive or negative. However, if they are not understanding and have an overwhelmingly negative response, and are unwilling to accept you for who you are, it is likely a red flag for the relationship in the long term. Although some people may be tempted to mask in a relationship if they really like the other person, this would be incredibly difficult to maintain long term and there could be significant consequences for your own well-being if you're constantly masking around the people you're supposed to trust.

When you first start a romantic or sexual relationship, the other person does not have to know everything about autism, ADHD and neurodivergence to be a good partner (likely that would be impossible anyway). But the key things to look out for is their willingness to learn about what your autism and ADHD mean for you, and their ability to accept you for who you are when you are not masking. If your partner does these, I'd say this is a positive sign of a loving and caring relationship (and you don't deserve any less than this!).

For some of us, we may end up in a relationship with another neurodivergent person. Again, this can be a positive, as we may be more likely to avoid the common misunderstandings that often occur between neurotypical and neurodivergent people. One autistic ADHDer shared their experiences with being in a relationship with another neurodivergent person and their partner's acceptance of who they are:

66 My first relationship has been my only relationship, and I've been with an amazing person for over ten years. I think I lucked out; he also has ADHD, and is much more accepting of the social, academic and mental health challenges I have, and is the greatest source of my support.

Being in a relationship with another neurodivergent person (or a similar neurotype) can be positive for some autistic ADHDers. This doesn't mean that every autistic ADHDer should only date other neurodivergent people, as sometimes our needs can also massively clash with each other. Still, it is important to recognise that for some of us, being in a romantic relationship with a fellow neurodivergent person can help with understanding and accepting each other (which is super important in romantic relationships).

What we each look for in a relationship will be unique, depending on our own personalities and preferences. However, it is vital that we are aware of potential key signs that the other person does not have good intentions in the relationship (also referred to as red flags), which can be harder to notice if the other person is a different neurotype from us or there are key differences in our social communication styles. Often these red flags will be related to not respecting our boundaries and consent, and trying to control other aspects of our lives (such as finances or our other relationships). It's important to know that these are not signs of a loving relationship (despite what they may say) and it is abusive. If you find yourself in this situation, then you may want to reach out to any support networks you have access to or supportive organisations to talk about your options for finding a way to safely leave if necessary.

Family dynamics

The dynamics within the family of an autistic ADHDer will be very different from one person to another depending on our situation. Some of us may have families that are supportive and understanding of our differences, while others may have had a more negative experience growing up, or no family involvement at all.

I think the biggest difference within our family relationships between when we are children and when we are adults is choice. By choice I mean we will have more autonomy to decide if we want to interact with our family or not, and how often we want to interact with our family – our neurodivergence may be a factor in this. For example, I enjoy spending time with my family but it can take up a lot of my social spoons (energy). So I may decide to spend a few hours with them rather than the whole day. By doing this, it means I can enjoy the quality time I spend with them, rather than being together all day and not being able to get the same enjoyment out of it due to tiredness. I often used to mask a lot around my family to manage longer social interactions with them, but by making this change it has been easier for me and there are fewer occasions where I am masking my exhaustion.

For many autistic ADHDers, there will be additional factors which will determine how we interact with our family members. Some of us may still be dependent on our families at the start of our adult lives, including still living with them. When this is the case, we may need to put boundaries in place to ensure we can have the privacy we need while still living at home. For myself, I had to put locks on the inside of my bedroom door to get the privacy I needed when living at home in my early twenties! Living at home when you come into adulthood isn't always easy, but as an adult you still have every right to establish boundaries when living in your family home so you can meet your own needs and have your privacy respected.

For other autistic ADHDers, families may play a smaller part in your life in adulthood for a variety of reasons such as living away from the family. However, if you had bad experiences in the past with your family, then you do not have to have a relationship with them at all (despite what society might tell us), and you may want to seek ways to move on from your family life.

Again, this is rarely an easy choice to make, and if you are in this situation, there is no right or wrong decision here (as each of our circumstances will be unique), it is about figuring out which choice is better for you in the longer term. If you do make changes with how you interact with your family going forwards, then you may want to make this a gradual process if you can, to reduce the stress that can often come with big and sudden changes for many autistic ADHDers. Nonetheless, the most important thing is doing it in a way that is safe and that works for you (taking into account your needs relating to both your autism and ADHD).

As we come into adulthood, some of our family dynamics will change, such as how often we see our family members and if we decide to start a family of our own. Other aspects of our family dynamics may not change at all, like our individual relations with family members, as these are often long-established relationships, e.g. sibling rivalry or overprotective parents. Ultimately though, as an adult, you should have more choice with how big or small a part family will play in your life going forwards.

Workplace interactions

A new type of relationship that we will come across as adults is with the people we work with, referred to as our work colleagues.

The relationships we have with our work colleagues will vary and navigating different personalities can be a significant factor in the workplace, in particular for autistic ADHDers (especially if most of our work colleagues are neurotypical). Across our working lives, we will likely get along a lot better with some work colleagues than others. Sometimes our relationships with work colleagues can develop into friendships if we get on well with them, while others will be workplace acquaintances only, where we are polite with them and can work together well, but we do not have interactions or spend quality time with them outside work.

Some people may even find their future partner at work (though this is never a guarantee!). If we do meet a partner at work, we may need to be careful of things such as power dynamics (if the person is a manager or somebody more senior in the organisation) and if the relationship will have a knock-on effect on your job. As each of these situations is unique depending on the dynamics of your relationship and your workplace's view on colleagues forming romantic relationships, it's hard to say exactly how things may play out (also workplaces often do not talk about these things directly). In some workplaces, it may not be a problem, whereas in others it might. My advice is just to be careful if you are not sure how your workplace may perceive a romantic relationship with another colleague.

We may also come across work colleagues who we have unpleasant interactions with or experience bullying from (unfortunately the risk of bullying does not end in school). Being autistic ADHDers, we may be more vulnerable to workplace bullying, as some people still have negative views and attitudes towards people who appear to be socially different. This doesn't mean to say this will happen at every workplace, but if it does, it may be a direct form of discrimination based on how others may respond to how our autism and ADHD present at work. These situations can be incredibly difficult if we have a work colleague who is being disrespectful and is upsetting us. Nonetheless, you will always have options of what you can do in these situations, including:

- Deciding to speak to a manager or another employee about what has been going on, to seek a resolution.
- Raise the issue with human resources (HR). HR is the part of an organisation that is responsible for employee relations.
- Others may feel they want to say something to the person directly, although this may feel risky.
- Seek advice from a trade union (organisations that represent workers' interests).
- Decide if you want to stay in this working environment, or start looking for a new job.

All of the above can be uncomfortable and feel nerve racking. Usually, people at work will try to speak to somebody first before deciding to leave their job (as this is often a big decision to make). However, if the situation between yourself and a work colleague (or colleagues) becomes unbearable and is significantly affecting you, then you can leave your job without speaking to others at work about the situation. Additionally, if you do raise the issue of workplace bullying and there is a lack of action and/or your concerns are not taken seriously, then this is a sign of a not-good employer! For many this would be a red flag, and at this point is when you might start to consider changing jobs.

If you need more specific advice about what to do if you find yourself experiencing workplace bullying, you could either speak with a person you trust for moral support, or a trade union for more practical advice about what you can do in the workplace and your rights as an employee.

One of the common unwritten rules of the workplace is the social expectations that come along with the job. Many workplaces (but not all) presume that all employees want to spend their lunch breaks with their colleagues and are always up for (at least most of the time) after-work drinks. While some of us may be okay with this, I am aware that many autistic ADHDers need time to decompress away from people to sustain their energy levels throughout the day.

It is by no means compulsory to spend your breaks and after-work hours with your colleagues, as that is your time and it is your right to spend that time however you like. Nonetheless, it is good to be aware that some work colleagues (unfairly in my opinion) may judge others who are not always around during work breaks or turn down socialising outside of work. How understanding people will be if you do not socialise during lunch breaks or after work will massively vary depending on the personalities of your colleagues (something we have very little control over!). However, if most people in your workplace are like this, and you need time away from others during your breaks and after work, then it could be that the workplace culture is not right for you.

Workplace culture is a concept that has been talked about much more in recent years, and refers to the common attitudes, views and expectations that create a unique working environment. As we are all unique, there isn't a magic formula that will help to create the perfect working environment for all autistic ADHDers (if only it were that easy!). However, we may find that certain workplace cultures may suit us and our neurodivergent needs more than others – I have certainly found this with the different places I have worked over the years.

As most people are not neurodivergent, this can often mean that workplace cultures are based on neurotypical norms, and can exclude autistic ADHDers (whether intentional by the organisation or not). Ideally, workplaces would have flexibility as part of their culture, so that autistic ADHDers can work in a way that best suits us and our needs. Some workplaces are better at this than others, and increasingly since the pandemic we are seeing flexibility becoming more common in the workplace. However, there are some workplaces that are not or cannot be flexible due to the nature of the work. Therefore, if flexible working is important for you, doing research during the application process on this can help you find out if the working environment at the organisation will suit you.

Another aspect of workplace culture that may also be an important factor to consider for autistic ADHDers is the formality of our work environment. For example, when I worked in education settings, interactions with my colleagues tended to be a lot more formal than when I worked for charities. Although interactions in the staff room in education were a lot more relaxed than interactions the classroom, so the level of formality can even vary within the same job!

You may find you develop your own preference for how you want to interact with people while at work. For example, some autistic ADHDers may prefer interacting in a formal way as they find it easier being in an environment where the social rules and expectations are clearly defined and it is one less thing to worry about. For other autistic ADHDers, working in an overly formal environment at work would require significant levels of masking, leading to burnout and not being able to sustain the job in the long term. And some autistic ADHDers may prefer working environments with minimal social interaction so they can focus on their work and not use up all their energy in the working day interacting with work colleagues and/or clients. So as you can see, there is wide variance in how workplace interactions can have an impact on us due to our divergence, even if we are all autistic ADHDers!

For me personally, I prefer working in environments which are not overly formal, as workplaces with strict social expectations require a significant amount of masking from me that is detrimental to my long-term well-being. Obviously, being in a position to choose a job based on the type of working environment and culture is quite a privilege (even though it shouldn't be). Sometimes we may be in a position in life where we have to take the first job we can get until we can find something else that is better suited to our needs – I have been there myself.

Learning that I was an autistic ADHDer in my early twenties certainly helped me realise what types of working environments would be detrimental to my well-being in the longer term. Once I had this better understanding I could plan for my next moves with employment, so that I could work towards getting a job I wanted in an environment that was more sustainable long term.

Finding the right type of employment and working environment can often take time and can be a case of trial and error, as sometimes you won't have a full idea of what it is like to work somewhere until you are an employee there. Almost nobody has a straightforward career throughout their whole lives, but it is worth thinking about some of the different things that your autism and/or ADHD may influence when it comes to finding the right job and working environment. If you are just finishing education and/or looking for your first job, then you may want to get some work experience in jobs that have different working environments, to figure out what type of workplace culture may suit you better. You could start this process by looking for internships or temporary jobs before committing to a permanent job.

5
Emotional well-being and mental health

Content warning: *Ableism, trauma and poor mental health*

Historically, autism and ADHD were thought to be 'mental health disorders' rather than neurotypes, although you may still come across people who hold this outdated view. As our understanding of neurodivergence has improved, autism and ADHD are now seen as neurotypes that describe developmental differences, meaning we are born with brains which work differently from neurotypical brains, rather than having something inherently wrong with us. However, many of us also either struggle with emotional well-being (how good we feel about ourselves) or have a co-existing mental health condition. Although there are likely many reasons for this, we cannot underestimate the impact that being different from others can have on autistic ADHDers' lives, especially in a world that is obsessed with everything being 'normal'. Dr Luke Beardon describes this well with his concept of **autism + environment = outcome**.

66 Many children develop psychiatric disorders as a result

> of their difficulties in life – this is not because they are autistic, but because of that equation: **autism + environment = outcome**. If the outcome is a psychiatric disorder (of which pathological anxiety states is a common one) then clearly the environment is 'wrong'. (Beardon, 2020, p. 127)

Although the quote above is specifically discussing autistic children, I believe that the concept also very much applies to autistic ADHDers as we come into adulthood, as many environments we enter will not be fully inclusive (due to society's lack of understanding and acceptance of neurodivergence). Unsurprisingly, we may become more vulnerable to experiencing distress if we are spending a significant amount of time in environments that are hostile to us. As one fellow autistic ADHDer put it:

66 I don't just want to say that all of my anxiety and depression was caused by neurodivergence, but I would say a good deal of it was just kind of the experience of growing up and feeling, you know, like you didn't belong.

For this reason this chapter will focus on our emotional well-being and mental health, including looking at environments we will likely spend a lot of time in during our early adulthood, such as university and the workplace, and the impact these can have on our mental health and well-being. I should point out that a significant proportion of the changes needed to make these environments inclusive for us is not within our individual control, and requires societal-level change (but more on that later on).

However, before we look at our emotional well-being and mental health in specific environments, it is important to understand how autistic ADHDers' well-being and mental health can differ from neurotypicals in terms of our expression of emotions (and how this is often misunderstood by others), internal thoughts and experience with trauma, along with rejection sensitivity. As our experiences often differ from most others, many standard (or generic) approaches or responses to our mental health will likely not be helpful, and sometimes even harmful. Which is why it is essential for us to start thinking about finding approaches that are better for us as neurodivergent individuals.

Emotions, expression and alexithymia

One of the key differences autistic ADHDers have from our neurotypical peers is how we experience and express our emotions. One example of this is when a neurotypical person experiences excitement, they may communicate this using their facial expressions by opening up their eyes so they appear wider while smiling widely. An autistic ADHDer, in contrast, may use stimming via repetitive movements with our hands or jumping up and down, or some of us may use creative avenues as a primary way to communicate our inner worlds through art, music or dance. Other autistic ADHDers may use augmentative and alternative communication (AAC) or writing to communicate their thoughts, feelings and emotions.

Additionally, many autistic ADHDers (along with other neurodivergent people) can experience difficulties in labelling our current emotions or explaining how we are feeling in a way most people around us can understand. This is known as alexithymia and is more common among neurodivergent people. Although people's experiences with alexithymia will vary, some of us can have challenges related to expressing and/or recognising all of our internal emotions and communicating them, whereas others can use language to label some emotions such as happy and sad, but find it more difficult to label when we are feeling emotions somewhere in between, such as satisfaction, anxiety or frustration. Some of us may also express our emotions through stimming, which others may not understand at first, or have to get to know us as individuals to understand that doing certain moves or stims is our way of expressing emotions.

For myself personally, I do not express most of my emotions on my face as most people would expect (unless I am experiencing emotions in their highest intensity or I am masking), and I prefer listening to music or sounds that reflect how I am feeling on the inside. I have a tendency to keep most of my emotions on the inside, but I do believe this is due to decades of masking, rather than being my most authentic way of expressing my emotions. So although I do relate to aspects of alexithymia, I am still trying to work out how much of my responses to emotions come from suppressing them for many years (rather than an inability to identify my emotions). So if you relate to descriptions of alexithymia and have masked your autism and ADHD, it is worth considering how masking may have impacted your emotional expressions and ability to identify your true emotions.

Unmasking is a process that I am still going through, even though I am now in my late twenties, which includes fully discovering my most natural way of communicating my internal world. Learning about being autistic and an ADHDer in my early twenties was certainly the first big step in working this out, as I now understand the reasons why I do not relate to how most other people express themselves or experience emotions. I am also not 'less than' for not having the same experiences as most other people, which is something I was made to feel guilty about before, such as finding a popular TV series boring when everybody else found it funny or entertaining, and thinking there was something wrong with me for not enjoying it like everybody else.

There are no wrong or right ways to express our emotions, but as most people communicate neurotypically, this can often mean that others misinterpret autistic ADHDers' emotions, in particular if they do not know us well or have little understanding of how neurodivergence affects how we communicate our emotions.

As I look back across my life so far, including before I knew I was neurodivergent myself, I have experienced people (well... mostly neurotypicals...) misreading my emotions a lot. One that continues to happen repeatedly is people thinking I am upset or there's something wrong when I am perfectly okay. I always find it happens when I least expect it and when I am minding my own business – neurotypicals can seem very strange!

Which brings me onto my next point nicely. The differences in communication between autistic ADHDers and neurotypical people can mean it does not come naturally for us to read neurotypical people's emotions, often expressed via their body language and facial expressions. Some of us may learn and find it easier over time to understand what neurotypical people are communicating, although this can often be exhausting and take a lot of effort. And some of us autistic ADHDers may find it difficult across our lives to fully interpret neurotypical communication.

However, as neurotypical people are the majority, many of us would have felt pressured into learning how neurotypical people communicate as a form of survival, without neurotypicals making an effort to understand how we communicate, or at least finding a middle ground for our communication styles. This can often mean we are putting significant amounts of effort into decoding what people are communicating in how they express their emotions, as many do not directly say what their true feelings are. Unsurprisingly, this is often tiring (as we are having to do this with most of our social interactions) and can lead to burnout after doing this continually for long periods of time.

Using tools that were mentioned earlier such as tracking spoons and energy accounting can help with managing how much we socialise to try and prevent burnout and for our well-being. At the same time, we are not responsible for the current inequalities that exist when it comes to neurotypical people making incorrect assumptions about how we as autistic ADHDers communicate and consequently are discriminated against. When we are discriminated against for not expressing our emotions in a neurotypical way, there will likely be an impact on our well-being and mental health, as we may no longer feel safe in certain environments or around certain people. We may want to seek emotional support from others we trust when we are discriminated against, or have some time away from others to regulate and do the things that make us happy.

We may need to make a decision about how we move forwards from this form of discrimination. What you decide to do will be up to you, depending on your personal circumstances and what you feel most comfortable doing to protect your emotional well-being, but some options are:

• Ask for accommodations and adjustments.

- Seek out environments which are safe for you to access and be in.
- Find new people to interact with, and distance yourself from people who are not willing to understand (if possible).
- Make a complaint (if the problem is with an organisation or public service).
- Find an advocate (that you can trust) who can provide the support needed in these situations.
- Consider if using schemes such as the sunflower lanyard may be helpful if similar situations happen again in the future.

Additionally, it is not just how we express our emotions that can be easily misunderstood, but also what we are responding to. If we're in a crowded supermarket or a busy restaurant, we may experience sensory overload, and have a flight response and leave the environment quickly. Although the reasons for this make complete sense for us, others may make ableist assumptions that we are 'overreacting' or being a 'drama queen', without an appreciation that we are having a completely different sensory experience to them. Likewise, this can work the other way too, where others may expect a reaction or response, and cannot understand why we may be more passive about what is happening. I remember once watching a film and everybody else around me was crying and felt a strong emotional response, whereas I didn't really feel anything towards it. They struggled to understand why I was not crying, and I didn't understand why they were at the time, a prime example of the double empathy problem!

The impact of these misunderstandings can vary from a situation where we feel awkward to one where our safety may be at risk, especially if we end up having a meltdown (a strong emotional response that is externalised) or a shutdown (an intense but internalised emotional response). During a meltdown, people may scream, shout or use physical outlets such as kicking in response to the distress they are experiencing, which is overwhelming. Whereas with a shutdown, we may be unable or have reduced ability to speak (if we normally do), or be unable to move or respond to people or events occurring around us.

Everyone will have their own ways of managing a meltdown or shutdown, but there are some things we can do that seem to be helpful for many autistic ADHDers. Having enough physical space away from others and not being interrupted can be the best form of self-regulation. Some of us may be extra sensitive to touch during a meltdown (more so than we usually are), and so should avoid coming into physical contact with others at this time. Other autistic ADHDers may need human interaction and a deep-pressure hug (or another form of deep pressure) to help with self-regulation. If there is any form of sensory stimuli that is causing distress, removing it (or moving somewhere else if possible) can also help reduce the likelihood of prolonging or escalating either the meltdown or shutdown.

After a meltdown or a shutdown, it is important we have the time and space needed to recover and process what has just happened. There are several possibilities of what can help, including spending time focusing on our interests, stimming and other forms of soothing movements, following our self-care routines or even curling up in a ball and hiding under a duvet for a few hours (my personal preference). Meltdowns and shutdowns are often an emotionally draining experience, so it is vital people around us respect our needs after these events, so that we can focus on feeling better within ourselves.

Although we can't always prevent meltdowns and shutdowns due to things being out of our control (like the time I had a very delayed flight, was hungry and tired and all the airport's food outlets were closed because it was the middle of the night!), sometimes we can help reduce them in future by reflecting back afterwards, when we are in a calmer place, to try and work out the reason they happened. If it is because we were in the supermarket at the busiest time of day leading to sensory overwhelm, it may be the case that next time we plan to go when it is less busy during their quieter times, or alternatively we start doing online shopping instead. If we get overwhelmed from social activities or from doing too many things in one day that require a high use of executive functioning, then using the tools such as tracking spoons or energy accounting that we mentioned earlier can help us plan our days around what we can manage, and prevent us becoming overwhelmed to the point of having a meltdown or shutdown.

Burnout

Another aspect of mental health and emotional well-being many autistic ADHDers experience is burnout. Burnout is when we run out of energy from working too much and not having enough time to rest. Although burnout is definitely not unique to autistic ADHDers, the frequency we experience burnout and the reasons why are different from neurotypicals. The term 'autistic burnout' has become more popular in recent years to describe these differences.

So how is autistic burnout different from regular burnout? The main difference is that often aspects of going about our daily lives drain a lot more of our energy than they do for neurotypical people. For example, experiencing sensory overload from going to the shops, or having to mask our way through different social interactions, can use up a significant amount of our available daily energy. As we use up a significant amount of our energy doing things that are seemingly effortless for neurotypical people (or at least which do not drain their energy levels at the same pace), additional pressures such as work, studying or family demands can be the thing that pushes us over the edge into an autistic burnout. In contrast for neurotypical people, burnout usually comes from having too much stress at work. I am yet to come across a neurotypical person who is burnt out from the regular demands of daily life, whereas this can very much be the case for autistic burnout.

As we are also ADHDers, sometimes we can end up getting into situations where we burn out more quickly too. Signing up to something new or taking on new responsibilities can be fun, and as ADHDers we often say yes in the moment. Although this is not necessarily a bad thing, it sometimes can lead us to saying yes and only later realising that we do not have the time or energy to take up this new thing alongside other commitments we have. It can also be hard for us to give something up or say no, especially if it is something we are enthused about and want to be involved with. Trying to fit new things in when we already have enough going on in our lives can be another way for us to all too easily slip into burnout.

As autistic ADHDers, it is important that we are aware of the aspects of both our autism and ADHD that may make us more likely to experience burnout. If we do not, this can lead to us having poorer mental health and well-being in the longer term. So what can we do to avoid burnout?

Tools we mentioned earlier such as tracking spoons or energy accounting can help us figure out how much energy we have each day and keep tabs on how we use it to avoid us becoming overwhelmed. Through this process we may realise that we are doing too much and need to set aside more time for relaxing. For others, it may be a case of cutting down our working hours, or accepting we only have the ability to work or study part time. Even among autistic ADHDers, we will all have different amounts of energy we can put towards doing certain activities, so it is important that we work out what works best for us and try not to compare ourselves to other neurodivergent people who are seemingly able to do a lot more than we can (on the surface at least).

Also the amount of energy we have will likely change over time. When we are not experiencing burnout, we will have the ability to do more things (but not too many, as we don't want to end up in burnout again!), whereas the number of spoons we may have available to us will be a lot less in the middle of a burnout. So it is important to factor this in when working out our energy levels.

Sometimes we need to accept that we need to withdraw from the world to prevent further burnout. I have had times where I had a few busy weekends in a row, which led to burnout, so I had to avoid socialising for fun for several months before I had the energy to start doing this again. Some of us may need to take extended breaks from work and studying to prevent or recover from a burnout, as it can last for months to years in some cases. This can be an incredibly difficult time, as we may be made to feel like a failure and there may be significant consequences for some of us if we experience long periods of burnout. However, stepping back can sometimes be the next step we need to take to look after ourselves, recover from burnout and start finding a way to live our lives without getting overwhelmed.

Trauma

We cannot talk about emotional well-being and mental health for autistic ADHDers without talking about trauma. Unfortunately, trauma is far too common among neurodivergent people due to the experiences and discrimination we have experienced growing up and in adulthood too.

Some examples of the types of discrimination we often face growing up (that can lead to trauma) include unfair or extreme levels of criticism in school (from both teachers and peers), which sometimes leads to exclusion. Or having neurotypical expectations placed on us by family members and receiving a harsh response for not meeting them. Or experiencing bullying and abuse in our communities, and being traumatised to the point where we do not feel safe leaving our homes.

Although trauma can be caused by a single significant event, this is not always the case; sometimes trauma comes from an accumulation of smaller events or setbacks that occur repeatedly over time. It's having to be subjected to these experiences over and over again that leads people to develop trauma. This type of trauma is sometimes referred to as CPTSD or complex-PTSD (although it is not a formally recognised diagnostic term). I'm not saying that every autistic ADHDer has experienced trauma in this way (or that this is a unique experience that just autistic ADHDers have). However, it is easy to see how this type of trauma can develop for autistic ADHDers who grew up in environments that were not understanding or accepting of our differences.

If we take the example of receiving extreme levels of criticism at school, often this can come from our peers in the form of social rejection or bullying for not 'fitting in', and from teachers assuming we're not capable due to not being able to thrive within a 'one size fits all' neurotypically designed curriculum. Many of us will have gone through experiences like these daily at school, five days a week, most weeks of the year, for over a decade. Although isolated comments and experiences like this would be less likely to have a big impact in the longer term, when it is constant for a significant amount of time like at school, it is easy to see why autistic ADHDers are more vulnerable to developing trauma as a result of discrimination – especially in an environment where we do not have the freedom to leave of our own free will (again like school as children). For myself, I unfortunately experienced this kind of trauma due to bullying and the attitudes of certain school staff over a long period of time. Although these may have been seen as 'smaller' incidents daily (sometimes they were not so small incidents), it was constant for nine years which lead to trauma. Thankfully as adults now, we do have the choice to leave if we are in a toxic work, college or university environment.

Autistic ADHDers can also experience trauma from single impactful events, and I will go as far as to argue that small, regular incidents over a long period of time will increase the likelihood of a bigger issue happening, making it more likely for us to also be traumatised by a singular event (alongside the trauma caused by the accumulation of smaller events). Although the trauma each autistic ADHDer may have will not be identical, I can say with confidence based on my lived experience and interviews that the trauma I have received over the years from being an autistic ADHDer has been the result of both an accumulation of smaller events and larger individual incidents, and that I am not the only autistic ADHDer who feels this way.

A more recent concept that has been developed by Fulton et al. (2020) is sensory trauma. Sensory trauma is when occurrences in daily life overwhelm our senses to the point they become traumatic for autistic people. Although sensory trauma is introduced as a concept to explain the sensory experiences of autistic people, it is also relevant to autistic ADHDers because we share the sensory experiences of many autistic people, in addition to the distractibility that comes from sensory stimuli for many ADHDers. Some of us autistic ADHDers will likely have our own hypersensitivities with sensory processing which may cause us to have a negative response or experience distress to the point that it is traumatic.

One example of a sensory trauma could be when previously you ate some food that sensory-wise was overwhelming (due to hypersensitivity to taste), so that every time you smell it now it makes you feel sick and have a negative reaction. Another could be sudden loud noises such as a siren on the road, or a loud bang from somebody dropping an object. Although trauma can often come from negative social interactions for autistic ADHDers, we should also consider how our environments and the unpleasant sensory experiences we may have in them can also contribute to trauma for some of us.

It is also worth mentioning that autistic ADHDers can become traumatised by other life adversities we may experience, unrelated (or at least not directly related) to being neurodivergent. Some of us may have a mixture of traumas where some are related to being an autistic ADHDer (in a world designed for neurotypicals) and others are not. So although it is useful to understand how your trauma may be rooted in your experiences as an autistic ADHDer, it is also important to consider how other experiences may have affected or contributed to any trauma alongside being neurodivergent.

If you do have trauma, you may be seeking answers on how to move forwards and reduce the suffering it can bring. As our experiences are unique, so will be the way we process our trauma and figure out how our needs can be met. For this reason, I will not recommend any one course of action when it comes to deciding on the best option for accessing trauma-related support. However, one thing I will say is that if you do access support, it is important to find out if they have experience of and knowledge about autism, ADHD and neurodiversity. More often than not, a lack of understanding of autism, ADHD and neurodiversity from people trying to support us can lead to our needs not being properly met, and can cause further harm (even if they are well intentioned). If you are seeking support for trauma, you may want to ask for recommendations from neurodivergent people, as they will be more likely to know who has the right knowledge and experience to provide the support we are looking for. There is also the option of accessing peer support, but the most important thing is that you do research into potential options and decide which one feels right or the best fit for you.

Rejection sensitivity

Rejection sensitivity is an intense emotional distress response to perceived or actual rejection. It is more commonly associated with ADHD, due to the differences ADHDers have with processing their emotions, and is an emotional response many autistic ADHDers experience throughout their lives. (Sometimes you may also come across rejection sensitivity referred to as rejection sensitivity dysphoria – RSD.)

As a result, we may avoid situations where there is potential rejection, such as not putting ourselves forward for opportunities or trying to develop relationships with others. Rejection sensitivity can also contribute to some of us becoming people pleasers, trying to avoid the potential emotional pain that can come from disagreements or potential conflict. Some autistic ADHDers also report experiencing perfectionism as a way to try and avoid criticism and rejection. One fellow autistic ADHDer I spoke with while writing this book briefly touched on how rejection affected them at work:

66 Rejection in a professional environment had bigger consequences than in my personal life, so I never felt like I could truly be myself in a work environment.

Although as autistic ADHDers we do process our emotions differently to most other people, we shouldn't put rejection sensitivity solely down to 'the ways our brains work'. As we live in a world that is not widely accepting for those of us thinking differently, we have likely experienced significantly more rejection than our neurotypical peers, whether when trying to make friends at school or applying for jobs and trying to get through the interview process. Our past experiences have often taught us to expect rejection (whether directly or indirectly). If we have experienced a lot of rejection in multiple areas of our lives (e.g. social, education, work), it is understandable why we may experience rejection sensitivity.

Rejection sensitivity is often very difficult and painful for the individual experiencing it, so it is understandable why some may want to seek specific support in this area to try and help improve their quality of life. Just as with trauma, there won't be a 'one size fits all' approach for autistic ADHDers when it comes to reducing the pain that rejection sensitivity can cause for us. However, some possible starting points or things worth considering when we experience rejection sensitivity are:

- If rejection sensitivity (or RSD) is a new concept for you, start to learn and find out more, to better understand what our brains may be going through when experiencing rejection, as it can feel isolating and sometimes scary if we do not know that what we are experiencing is related to rejection sensitivity (you've already started this one by reading this section of the book!).
- Try to identify when we are experiencing rejection sensitivity to see if there are any clear patterns or triggers. Often this can be related to past experiences and traumas (but not always).

- If we have identified what contributes to our strong emotional responses to feelings of rejection, then it is worth thinking about the reasons why these are triggers. Sometimes it can be our brain's way of telling us what is important to us (which is why we may worry about it so much), or a way of keeping us safe emotionally from things that may have hurt us in the past.
- Think about what we can do to make our feelings of rejection less painful and reduce how debilitating they can be. This will be unique to each of us, but some examples could include thinking about what is calming and self-soothing for us (such as stimming), or whether there is a person we can trust and speak with to provide reassurance when experiencing rejection sensitivity.

Some autistic ADHDers may want support and to go through the steps mentioned above with a professional such as a therapist. If you decide to do this, make sure they have a strong understanding of rejection sensitivity within the context of autism and ADHD, as standard approaches to mental health often fail to take into account our needs.

For myself, rejection sensitivity is something I experienced a lot and internalised most of the time. Through my own self-reflection and learning more about rejection sensitivity, I have been able to better understand why I had a strong reactionary response to rejection. Although this has not entirely removed rejection sensitivity from my life, it has helped me become more compassionate towards myself (and less self-critical) when I do experience rejection, and has made the negative emotions I experience less intense.

Dealing with neurotypical norms around emotional well-being and mental health

I suspect it won't come as a surprise to many reading this that neurodivergent people can often experience poor mental health. Although there are often a variety of reasons for this, our marginalisation and being misunderstood repeatedly within a world that expects us to be neurotypical undoubtedly plays a role here. Also, often the responses people have when we are experiencing distress or struggling with our mental health are designed around the assumption that we experience the world neurotypically. One autistic ADHDer shared how the lack of support for neurodivergent people has made things more difficult for them:

66 The main challenge has actually been trying to get the support for my mental health, more than the actual mental health itself, because my mental health wouldn't get worse if getting the support wasn't such a challenge. And the fact that getting the support is a challenge as a neurodivergent person means that the mental health just gets worse.

A classic example of this is cognitive behavioural therapy (CBT), which is often seen as a first step among medical professionals for anybody who is experiencing a high level of anxiety. Another fellow autistic ADHDer shared their experience accessing mental health care including CBT.

66 And also just the usual CBT doesn't work. It has to be adapted for ADHD, has to be adapted for autism, and it has to be undoubtedly adapted for ADHD and autism.

The combination of CBT often not being a neurodivergent-friendly approach and a lack of understanding of our differences means that the services we are told to access when we need support often cannot provide genuine support regardless of how good (or bad) the professional's intentions may be. Although some of us have found adaptations to different types of therapies helpful, it is by no means a solution for us all.

If you do decide to seek mental health treatment and support, it is always worth asking what experience they have with supporting neurodivergent people, and how they can adapt the support they provide to meet your unique needs. Due to the past experiences many neurodivergent people, including autistic ADHDers, have had with mental health professionals, it is common for us to seek out mental health professionals who are autistic and/or ADHDers themselves. Increasingly, professionals are being more open about their lived experiences in addition to their professional experience, so if you would feel more comfortable being supported by somebody with similar lived experience to yourself, it may be worth doing research to see if this is an option.

A serious note here: there may be times when for some of us our choice is taken away by mental health professionals if they feel we are experiencing a crisis, for example, being admitted onto a psych ward. Just because this can happen to autistic ADHDers does not mean it is right. In cases where neurodivergent people do end up having decisions relating to their care taken away from them, often this is due to professionals misunderstanding our autism, ADHD and our needs relating to this, meaning that sometimes meltdowns are triggered in a way which could have been avoided. Also if we do not have the right support in place in our communities, then we may also become more vulnerable to a crisis and ending up in this situation. If this does happen to you, then it is always worth seeking legal advice where you live to challenge the decisions that have been made by others and to gain your autonomy back.

Professionals are not the only ones who might take a neurotypical approach to mental health care: quite often many non-professionals will give out generic mental health advice too, from a family member telling us to 'just relax' to a stranger on the internet creating infographics telling us the mental health benefits of taking a bath and lighting some candles. Although this may work for some, it certainly won't fully address how we experience our mental health as autistic ADHDers.

If it is strangers trying to give us mental health advice, then we can ignore them and not engage with what they are saying. However, if it is people closer to us, then we may need to create a boundary about them giving us mental health advice. It is important to remember that we do not have to take advice from anybody just because they are a family member, friend or someone with experience supporting others with their mental health. We can ask questions and challenge if we do not agree, especially if they are not taking our autism and ADHD into account. It is solely up to us who we can trust when discussing our mental health (despite what others may have told us in the past). Some autistic ADHDers find it more helpful to engage with peer support rather than turning to more traditional mental health services.

Many approaches to mental health operate on a 'one size fits all' approach, meaning that any differences from what is considered 'normal' lead to our needs not being fully met as autistic ADH-Ders. At a minimum, we may need adaptions to mental health care, if we feel a service is capable of supporting us, but the most important thing is we do not have to accept support if it will not make a positive difference in our lives. If your autism and/or ADHD has been misunderstood by people who are trying to support your mental health needs, then you are certainly not alone. If they are not prepared to make the adjustments you need, you disagree with their approach or they are disrespectful towards you for being neurodivergent, then these people are unable to support us. It should be our choice to seek out support, but at the same time, if we are offered support, it is important to ask questions and ensure they understand all of our needs.

Misdiagnosis and missed diagnosis

Another experience that is fairly common among autistic ADH-Ders is being misdiagnosed with a mental health condition, most commonly (but certainly not limited to) anxiety, depression, borderline personality disorder and emotionally unstable personality disorder (although for some, these may co-exist alongside autism and ADHD). One of the reasons for misdiagnosis is people not fitting exactly into the current boxes for autism and ADHD, meaning they receive only one diagnosis, none at all or a completely different one entirely. Also, we often only come into contact with professionals who do diagnostic assessments when we have a problem or are experiencing significant distress. The potential consequence is that they may only focus on what is going on with us now, rather than considering our experiences across life so far. Both autism and ADHD are developmental in nature, meaning that the signs we are autistic ADHDers are present from early childhood (even if it wasn't recognised at the time). So if professionals do not decide to ask questions about our childhood and development, there is an increased chance that autism and ADHD will be missed.

As mentioned in Chapter 1, the diagnostic criteria for both autism and ADHD were formed based on a very narrow demographic, meaning clinicians often will have a bias (either conscious or unconscious) as to who should receive a diagnosis of autism and/or ADHD. This is not to mention the additional influence that comes from stereotypical views and tropes of autism and ADHD. Although you would expect clinicians and professionals to know the difference between a stereotype and actual neurodivergence, many of us who decided to seek a diagnosis (or if our parents took us when we were younger) came across this bias and were gatekept from receiving a diagnosis, including myself.

Another result of being autistic ADHDers is that we are not recognised as having either autism or ADHD, due to not fitting exactly into the neat boxes for each as designed by professionals. One of the autistic ADHDers I spoke with shared how their autism meant that they did not present typically as an ADHDer:

66 But I don't typically behave as if I've got ADHD. It's more in my mind than, like, physically, which is interesting. I don't like bounce off the walls. I don't go on runs for like ten miles or work all day and then be able to go out all night and all that. But for me, it's more sort of my mind is just constantly active.

Although I am aware that not every ADHDer is bouncing off the walls and is full of energy 24/7, the fact we are autistic too will mean that our ADHD will not present in a way people fully expect. The same is often true for our autism, meaning we do not present as a typical autistic person due to our ADHD. As a result, we may be missed entirely and not recognised as neurodivergent at all. People may apply negative labels to us that are not accurate. Or we may not have the option to pursue a diagnosis, even if it will open up the right support for us.

Although I did not receive my own autism diagnosis until my twenties, I was misdiagnosed as a younger child with a language disorder when I was first assessed for autism. As this was during the late 1990s, hardly any girls were recognised as autistic at the time, and I can't help but think that my gender was a reason for the misdiagnosis, as I do not present in a stereotypically autistic way on the surface. It has only been within the last few years that professionals have started to realise that women and girls are autistic too, and that we are not the odd anomaly among autistic people. The same is true for ADHD, as more women are receiving a diagnosis in later life, along with people from other marginalised backgrounds, which the diagnosticians and their criteria had often previously ignored.

For myself, I did not even think ADHD could be a possibility until I started engaging with neurodivergent people and started to learn about what ADHD was actually like from ADHDers themselves, and particularly autistic ADHDers, as I increasingly found my ways of thinking and experiences were very closely aligned with this. Looking back now I suspect that also being an ADHDer meant that I did not receive an autism diagnosis earlier on, and ADHD was not on anybody's radar!

I suspect a fair number of my fellow autistic ADHDers have been misdiagnosed or missed at some point, which is why this issue cannot be ignored when discussing emotional well-being and mental health. The consequences of both misdiagnosis and missed diagnosis can vary, but can be significantly negative for some of us, especially for those who end up as inpatients on psychiatric wards (when this all too often turns out to be the worst place for us). For some, pursuing and receiving an autism and ADHD diagnosis (and potentially removing inaccurate diagnoses we may have received along the way) means access to the right support, which can reduce our suffering and overall improve our emotional well-being and mental health.

The decision to pursue a diagnosis for both autism and ADHD should always be our choice, as the impact a diagnosis can have in our individual lives will be unique to our circumstances. Even if you have been misdiagnosed previously, it doesn't necessarily mean getting an autism and/or ADHD diagnosis now will be the right solution for you. If you are unsure about whether you want to pursue an autism and/or ADHD diagnosis, you can use the guide in Chapter 1, 'Introducing autism and ADHD', to assist you in weighing up the pros and cons of diagnosis. However, I fully understand that a number of autistic ADHDers will have trauma and mistrust from medical and mental health services (especially if you were misdiagnosed previously), and that coming back into contact with psychological services (or similar) might do more harm than good. So if this is the case for you, please know that you do not have to put yourself through diagnostic assessment if it will negatively impact your safety and well-being.

Co-existing mental health conditions

Although a fair number of us autistic ADHDers will have been misdiagnosed along the way, it is also important to acknowledge that many of us do have mental health conditions alongside autism and ADHD. For example, somebody may also experience depression or trauma as well as being an autistic ADHDer. Having mental health conditions in addition to being autistic ADHDers can create additional challenges, as one autistic ADHDer shared:

66 Dealing with depression on top of ND symptoms (still with no support from my family) makes it almost twice as hard.

However, if we do reach out or end up under the care of mental health services, sometimes we may receive a diagnosis which may be accurate, but only reflects part of what we are experiencing or the challenges we are currently facing. As another autistic ADHDer shared, they felt the labels of anxiety and depression didn't fully describe how they were experiencing the world:

66 But I always knew deep down that it was not just anxiety and depression. That there was something else underneath.

I also related to the quote above a lot. For years I had been told I was 'just experiencing anxiety' and 'maybe depression'. Although I didn't disagree with these statements, it had come to a point during my early adult years where I began to think that there was something more significant going on than just anxiety and/ or depression. Although I had no idea at the time what exactly this was, I later came to learn that I am autistic and later still an ADHDer too. Although learning about my neurodivergence did not automatically solve all my problems overnight (if only!), it did help to understand that the reason why I was struggling so much was due to decades of unrecognised and unmet needs due to both autism and ADHD and trying to survive in a world that was not designed for a brain like mine. It also helped me to understand masking and to see how this contributed towards both my anxiety and depression.

If we do have metal health conditions in addition to autism and ADHD, it is important that the people around us (or support-ing us) have awareness of how our differences may affect how we present. For example, many of us will have different facial expressions and use of body language than most when we are experiencing our emotions. Therefore, it is essential that the people around us are aware of what our happiness or sadness may look like, as this could be quite different from what they expect. Also, it is vital that anybody providing mental health support understands what may cause us more distress, and that this can differ from people who are neurotypical. Examples of this include increased anxiety from overwhelming sensory stimuli potentially leading to a meltdown or shutdown, and rejection sensitivity perhaps being a factor in why we are experiencing depression. The exact reasons as to why we may be experiencing distress will be unique to each of us and any past traumas we may have been through.

If these differences with our mental health are not considered and accommodated, this can lead to harm (whether intended by the other person or not). So it is vital, if we are being supported by others, that we have choice and autonomy over who these people are and that we can have two-way conversations with them about our needs and how we need to be supported. As the power imbalance between professionals and patients in more traditional mental health settings can create barriers when it comes to conversations about support, we may need to seek out an advocate to have our voices heard and respected.

Education and mental health

Education has likely been a significant part of your life up until now, and many fellow autistic ADHDers reading this may still be in education themselves. Whether we are coming towards the end of school, or are in the middle of college or university, it is likely we will experience ups and downs with our mental health. Periods with lots of exams, for example, are likely to be much more stressful than other times in the academic year.

I suspect that many autistic ADHDers will have had negative experiences in school, which likely worsened our mental health. However, if education is done right, it can be a positive aspect of our lives. If we are in an educational environment where all our needs are met, we enjoy what we are studying and have good relationships with teachers and peers, education can be a source of happiness, fulfilment and personal growth. Although most of my educational experiences were negative, this changed when I had more choice in what I studied and where. Meaning I could choose the best options for myself, rather than others making all of the educational choices for me in an authoritarian environment (aka school).

I do recognise though that the majority of schools, colleges and universities still have a way to go to be fully inclusive for neuro-divergent people. Although I would love fully inclusive education to be a reality for autistic ADHDers, the exclusion and lack of understanding and accommodations means that we often pay the price with our mental health. So if our mental health is suffering due to education, what can we do?

The first thing to consider is whether there are any practical changes that can be made if accessibility is an issue such as to the sensory environment or how things are communicated by a teacher or instructor. If you wish to ask for any changes, it can be helpful to plan what you need to ask for in advance of speaking with your school, college or university, so that you are able to tell them everything you need in one go. As this can be nerve racking for some of us to do alone, it may be worth asking somebody we trust or finding an advocate to help us ask and get the adjustments we need. Depending on where you are studying, there sometimes can be specific mental health support that you can access via your school, college or university. So if you are struggling it is worth seeing if your institution provides any mental health support you can access.

However, sometimes adjustments can only go so far, and mental health support that schools, colleges and universities provide (if any) can be limited due to funding. Often, there can be bigger and more significant issues which cannot be quickly resolved. Sometimes the educational environment can be too hostile for us, and it may be a case of needing to change where we are studying, or deciding whether accessing education is the best next step for our mental health. Again, this change doesn't always have to mean starting at a new school – it could be that any school would be too inaccessible, meaning that it wouldn't make much difference to your mental health if you moved from one school to another. It could be a case of exploring other options that may be available to you such as home education or remote learning.

Once we finish compulsory education, things are slightly different as we can choose whether or not to continue studying. If our mental health is being significantly impacted by staying in education (or by continuing to study at the same institution or course) then the best thing might be to take a break, or even to drop out. I know this will not be a popular opinion with everyone, but your mental health and well-being is worth more than a certificate or diploma. Remember that you can always go back to education later on if you wish, and sometimes to survive, we may need to focus on our health (both physical and mental) before we can pursue our educational goals. It is also okay if you decide never to return to education due to the impact it has had on your mental health. There will always be other opportunities outside of formal education – going through further and higher education is only one of many different options.

Work and mental health

As we come into adulthood, for some of us autistic ADHDers work will likely be something on our mind. Starting our first job or starting a career can be a huge change in itself from full time education, which can consequently impact our mental health. Additionally, if we are in a work environment that is ill-suited to our needs, this can be a significant detriment to our mental well-being (trust me, I have experienced this more than once, it can truly take over your life in a bad way). Don't worry though, we will go through possible ways of navigating the workplace while looking out for our mental health too.

Things that we have covered in previous chapters such as our working environments, how flexible a workplace is, the relationships with our colleagues and if we are employed or self-employed are all factors that will influence our mental health at work. How these factors may affect us will vary, as we are all individuals who will be in different working environments across our lives. However, if one or many of these factors is affecting us at work, then our mental health will likely be negatively impacted. So if we find ourselves in this situation, what can we do?

Similarly to when we are in education, one option is to speak to our employer to ask about any adjustments we may need in the workplace that will help us to maintain our well-being. Some examples of adjustments that may help maintain good mental health are changes to our working hours, adjustments to the environment we are working in (e.g. if a light is too bright, or a noise is too loud) or more flexible options when it comes to working from home. Having adjustments or understanding from our employer is often essential for us sustaining our work in the long term. Especially if we are in a job we like (or even love); it is vital that we have these conversations with our employer, so that we don't burn out and are forced to leave work due to not having our neurodivergent needs met.

If this is something that you are not confident in approaching your employer with, then you can always seek advice from a union about how to approach these situations, or to support you with discussions you may want to have around any adjustments you may need. When it comes to issues with relationships at work impacting our mental health, we can go to our employer to try to resolve this if we wish, but it is often not as straightforward as making a few simple changes. We explored workplace bullying in Chapter 4, as well as the full options you have if you find yourself in this situation.

My working experience so far has been a mix of jobs I really enjoyed and others not so much. I have also had to leave work

I enjoyed because the workplace could not meet all my needs. So although the work itself was appealing to me, the inability to be supported in that workplace meant that my mental health suffered significantly, and in the end it was a choice between either quitting immediately with no other job to go to, or only staying in the job until I could find another one that could meet my needs. I now prioritise finding an employer who is willing to provide adjustments, just as much as enjoying the work itself, as without doing this, I would more than likely fall into the same problem again.

So if you approach your employer and they are unable to accommodate your needs, then it is okay to start looking for another job where this is possible, and will be better for your overall mental health. For some of us, our workplaces may be compromising our mental health to such an extent that we cannot wait to find another job and we may have no choice but to have to quit immediately. Again this is always an individual choice, but unfortunately for many there will be financial consequences to quitting with no backup plan. If you find yourself in this situation, it is important to weigh up the pros and cons of doing this based on your individual situation, so that you can make an informed choice about whether you should quit now or wait.

For others, it may be the case that our mental health prevents us from working or taking another job. This could be on a temporary basis, or a permanent one depending on our own mental health needs and how much these will affect us across our lives. The support available to you if you are unable to work will vary massively depending on where you live, and may change over time, so I am unable to say exactly what support you may be able to access. However, what you can do is research the support available where you live – or if this is too much right now there are often charities/organisations who can help you navigate accessing the support you need, or you could ask somebody you trust enough to help you research your options.

6
Identity and acceptance

❝ When actually we're not broken. We're just different.

A big part of growing into adulthood is learning more about ourselves and trying to figure out who we are as individuals. Every young adult will go through this process – but for autistic ADHDers there are additional layers, as part of this process will involve figuring out how much of our own identity comes from being neurodivergent. Depending on who you ask, some autistic ADHDers see their neurodivergence as a core part of who they are and find it impossible to separate their neurodivergence from their personal identity, while others do not feel that their autism and/or ADHD is part of their identity, and see their neurodivergence as just a diagnosis or just their neurotype which does not define who they are. And there are other autistic ADHDers who view their neurodivergence as somewhere in the middle between an identity and a label. Our views on being neurodivergent will likely impact on our own self-acceptance. Whether we view our neurodivergence positively or not will often be informed by our past experiences. If we view ourselves negatively for being neurodivergent it can make self-acceptance a lot harder. Later in this chapter we will consider how we can become more self-accepting as neurodivergent people.

Going through our late teen years and coming into our early twenties is often a significant time in terms of learning to understand who we truly are as individuals. During this period, we will likely experience challenges (some of which likely related to being neurodivergent) as we pursue further education, form romantic relationships and discover what we want to do with our lives. If I am being honest, this is rarely straightforward for most people, but being autistic ADHDers, it can be harder to figure out our place in the world due to the additional barriers and setbacks we will face along the way. That's why in this chapter we will go through different aspects of coming into adulthood as an autistic ADHDer while trying to figure out who we are. We will start off by looking at how figuring out who we are relates to being neurodivergent, followed by how to build a life around our own neurodivergent needs. We will then take a look at what other aspects of our lives may inform our identity (in addition to our neurodivergence).

In the second part of this chapter, we will begin to look at neurodiversity as a concept, how it relates to the social model of disability and the impact this can have on our self-perception as neurodivergent people. We will then close by focusing on the positives that can come from being neurodivergent and how to work towards self-acceptance as neurodivergent people, which is not a straightforward task for many of us, but is not impossible either.

Finding out who you are and how this is related to your neurodivergence

One question many autistic ADHDers often have when coming to understand themselves better is how much does our neurodivergence form a part of our self-identity? Okay, we may not ask ourselves this exact question, but during our early adult years, we will likely think about how we are experiencing autism and ADHD (as this will differ from our school years), and if our neurodivergence forms part of our identity and who we are as a person. If I could only give one answer to this question, it would be 'How long is a piece of string?' as it will vary between every autistic ADHDer you ask. However, some of the autistic ADHDers I spoke with while writing this book did share with me how they view their identity in relation to their neurodivergence:

66 Yeah, but I do feel like it. It does affect like, I don't know, it's like it's not the only thing about me, but it's also something you can't remove. Like even things down to like what some of my interests are. Or the things I'm good at – I think it's like the whole structure of the brain it affects literally everything.

66 A lot of my neurodivergence is a core part of who I am, and I'm still sorting out how much are traits of my personality, and how much are symptoms from being ND.

66 I do have autism and ADHD. Yeah, it is a very huge part of me. How I live my day-to-day life, who I am, how I understand my identity.

66 Part of my identity? Well of course it's supposed to be because without it, what would I be? I would be a totally different person so yeah course it is. Whether it is significant I don't know because my mood can distort that at times but it is part of my identity.

Interestingly the majority of the autistic ADHDers I spoke with seem to have a similar view of how their neurodivergence is a significant part of their identity, but not their whole identity. I would agree with this myself, as besides being neurodivergent I am also a writer, daughter, sister, aunty, cat mum/crazy cat lady, advocate and Simmer (somebody who plays *The Sims...* a lot!). So there is more to me than just being an autistic ADHDer. However, since the depth of some of my interests comes from my autism, I think it would be highly unlikely that I'd love *The Sims* as much as I do, or be so devoted to my cat (yes, my autism certainly makes me a better cat mum). Also being an autistic ADHDer impacts how I interact with my family members and other important people in my life – it's interwoven with the other parts of my identity and I cannot separate my neurodivergence from who I am (which is why I say it is a big part of my identity). However, while the views shared here on neurodivergence in relation to identity are all quite similar, this will not be the case for every autistic ADHDer. Some will feel that being neurodivergent does not define them, but it is an addition to who they are. It is also worth mentioning there are no right or wrong ways to be neurodivergent, and autistic ADHDers aren't superior if they do feel their neurodivergence defines them.

Some of us may feel we already know or do not need to know how much our neurodivergence informs our identity. However, if we have spent a lifetime (up until now) masking a lot of the time, there can be extra challenges in figuring out who we are. As we often present outwardly based on what we have observed from our own culture's societal norms, masking can take away our ability to learn about ourselves and understand our identity as we mature.

In addition to this, if we did not know we were neurodivergent until we were in our teens or older, this lack of knowledge can massively impact our self-view and identity, as we won't be able to understand why we feel and experience the world differently from most people around us. And when we do find out, to suddenly have an explanation or label to explain our difference can be a shock (especially if it was unexpected). And when we are new to learning about autism and ADHD, we may have no knowledge of it at all, or if we do, there's a reasonable chance it's based on negative stereotypes (as there is still a lot of misinformation about autism and ADHD in the mainstream media) that do not align with our reality. There can also be a lot of emotions when discovering you are autistic and/or an ADHDer later on. Some will have positive feelings of validation that they now have an explanation for why they are different to most other people. Others may feel upset with the confirmation that they are not neurotypical (or 'normal') and grieve over the times where they were discriminated against or had unmet needs related to their autism and ADHD. The reality is that most people will experience a mix of these emotions.

Intersecting identities

Along with being autistic ADHDers, many of us will also be part of other communities based on our culture, ethnicity, sexuality or gender, which will also affect our identity and how we navigate the world as neurodivergent people. This is often referred to as intersecting identities or intersectionality. Having intersectional identities means that autistic ADHDers rarely have identical experiences to each other, even if we can relate to certain aspects of sharing the same neurotype.

When speaking with the autistic ADHDers who have contributed to this book, some of them shared their experiences of being neurodivergent along with other parts of their identity. One opened up about their experiences as a queer person and trying to navigate how much of their identity comes from being part of marginalised communities:

66 I think this happens when you're any kind of marginalised person that's still kind of coming to grips with it, like whether it's because... I think like with queerness this sometimes happens. It is like, well, okay, I'm this thing, but I'm not. I'm not going to make everything about me. And then you kind of realise one day it is a lot of you even if you don't want it to be.

As you can see, we sometimes experience conflicting ideas between how much we want an aspect of our lives to define our identity and how much in reality it does in our daily lives. If we experience conflicting thoughts related to how much our identity comes from our marginalisation, it can create additional pressures. Queerness is just one example of how our experiences as autistic ADHDers can intersect with other aspects of our lives. Another autistic ADHDer shared how their neurodivergence was received in their community:

66 My rigidly logical nature meant that I couldn't grasp much of the figurative language, sarcasm or subtlety that makes up the heart of our culture, and I was often made fun of for 'not being black enough'.

Autistic ADHDers come from a variety of communities, but the experiences and people's responses to our difference will vary depending on the cultural norms that surround us. For the autistic ADHDer above, this meant being told they were not 'black enough' when it came to the sarcasm and humour used in their community.

Being told that we are not similar enough to other members of our communities can be hurtful, especially when our authentic selves are not appreciated or when being visibly neurodivergent comes with stigma. This can negatively impact our identity and self-view, as we may be told often (directly or indirectly) that we do not 'fit into' the expectations within our communities and cultures, meaning we can feel isolated and made to feel like outsiders in places we are supposed to belong.

In addition to this, we may also be around others who have negative attitudes towards neurodivergent people, which is something that one autistic ADHDer discussed:

66 Talking about anything related to mental health was deeply frowned upon, outside of a Christian or spiritual lens. Any kids that had autism or disabilities were called 'special needs', in whispered and pitied tones.

Coming from a cultural and/or religious background that has stigma around autism, ADHD and disabilities can be an isolating experience and create additional need or pressures to mask, even around some of the people closest to us in our lives. Even if autistic ADHDers want to be more open about their neurodivergence with those who share the same religion or culture, there could be potentially significant risks to this. Autistic ADHDers who experience this may be forced into hiding their neurodivergence and be unable to openly explore their identity as an autistic ADHDer, which can limit our understanding of ourselves as we come into adulthood. For many autistic ADHDers, figuring out how much being neurodivergent forms our personality and who we are as people is part of the process of becoming an adult. Having a safe space to do this is vital, but depending on our circumstances, it may be difficult to find space to safely do this within the communities we grew up in and/or are a part of.

I also think that this is part of the reason why the online neurodivergent spaces are becoming more popular and is always growing. Many autistic ADHDers do not feel accepted, understood or valued by the people within their daily lives, and so the only place they have access to others who are openly neurodivergent is on social media. Although social media will always come with its risks and pitfalls, for some of us it can be a lifeline to learning about autism and ADHD in a more positive light and be a step towards understanding who we are and learning to accept ourselves as neurodivergent people.

For myself, being a women has undoubtedly affected my experiences as an autistic ADHDer. I always felt very different to most groups of women and I didn't relate much to how most women I knew socialised and interacted with each other, even though I assumed I would be able to relate to them just because we were all women. However, discovering I am both autistic and an ADHDer made me realise that I was not a stereotypical woman, and it was okay that I did not fully relate to women who fit the mould. In this sense it has helped relieve the pressure I felt to be a neurotypical woman, and allowed me to understand why I could not relate. I now know it is okay that I don't fit the stereotype based on my gender, and that I can find happiness without thinking I have to be a certain kind of woman.

How we navigate having multiple aspects of our identity as

autistic ADHDers and/or being part of more than one marginalised group will partially depend on our own experiences within our communities. However, it is worth trying to find people who can fully accept you for who you are, especially if you are feeling hostility from some people. Also, some neurodivergent people have increasingly been creating safe spaces for those who are also part of another marginalised group, e.g. spaces specifically for neurodivergent trans people. A group created specifically for people sharing the same intersecting identities as yourself may be a good place to seek out those who better understand your experiences, perhaps for the first time. Some groups may meet in person, while others may be online, but it is worth doing your research to see what groups or safe spaces you might be able to access.

Also, if you cannot find a space like this that is accessible or right for you yet, then you could explore the option of creating one for people with similar or shared identities. Just because a space that we are seeking doesn't exist yet doesn't mean we are stuck. This also doesn't have to be something you do by yourself (which can seem daunting) – if you want to create a space specifically for neurodivergent people, it would be worth reaching out to people who may be interested in being part of the group and seeing if they'd like to help you create it.

The social model, neurodiversity and disability

For many people, their views and understanding of autism and ADHD comes from medicine, and this viewpoint is referred to as the 'medical model'. The medical model solely focuses on the negatives and views everything associated with autism and ADHD as a 'deficit', and disregards everything else about a person outside of those negative labels the medical model is focused on fixing. Naturally, if these are the only descriptions we come across of autism and ADHD, it's not likely that we would have a positive self-view or be self-accepting.

However, outside of the medical model, other viewpoints have been developed which can be helpful when coming to understand who we are and developing our self-acceptance. One of these viewpoints is the social model by Mike Oliver (2013), which acknowledges the systemic barriers and stigma disabled people in our society face, unlike the medical model which focuses solely on what a person cannot do. An example of what the social model can look like in reality for autistic ADHDers is noting that exams have strict time limits, which puts many of us at a disadvantage who need more time for processing our thoughts and being able to fully express our abilities. Somebody at some point made a decision to set time limits, and as a result, the system created a barrier (that didn't need to be there) for many neurodivergent people trying to succeed in exams.

This is just one example of how the system often is not designed for autistic ADHDers, which is a form of discrimination, and can come along with blame and stigma aimed towards us for simply not fitting into neurotypical norms. Often this makes us feel inferior and can have a real effect on our self-esteem in the longer term. So it is important to remember that this is not our fault (which society likes to tell us) and that many things are set up with the assumption that we all experience the world in the same neurotypical way.

One of the autistic ADHDers who I interviewed reflected on the impact self-blame can have on our self-esteem and how understanding their ADHD and autism helped to ease the amount of blame they used to put on themselves:

> Yeah. I think that's really important because I feel like if you're not in that place (you want to be in), quite often, you go to like, self-blame. And then that's where the thoughts don't, you know, like I'm worthless. I'm not as good as other people, like all those types of thoughts come in. So I think to have that level of awareness of yourself – that it isn't because like you're deficient or whatever, it is because oh, I've got ADHD (and autism). So I need to do this (rather than following expected norms). To kind of satisfy that need. I think it's a really kind of refreshing way to look at it.

One viewpoint that was created by autistic activists (Botha et al., 2024) is neurodiversity. Neurodiversity is the recognition of the natural diversity of human brains, and that just because somebody is different from what our society deems 'normal', does not mean they are less than those who are neurotypical. Increasingly, some autistic ADHDers have been starting to view their neurodivergence through this lens (rather than the medical view), as it does not demonise our whole way of being as a problem that needs to be fixed. It is often society valuing one way of thinking over another that can make life more challenging for autistic ADHDers. Although neurodiversity as a concept does not solve all the problems we may come across, it can be a helpful way to start viewing ourselves more positively when working on self-acceptance – it can help us to see that the differences or struggles we do have do not mean that we are bad people.

The double empathy problem is another concept which challenges the view of neurological differences as disorders (as mentioned in Chapter 4), and can provide a fresh perspective on social interactions that we feel we either 'failed' at or were 'blamed' for a miscommunication. The double empathy problem explains that two people who have very different ways of communicating with each other will likely have some difficulties in understanding each other, and that one way of communicating is not superior to another. As autistic ADHDers, we are part of a social minority compared to neurotypicals, meaning we often unfairly get the full blame for any miscommunications. Communication is always a two-way street, and the reality is that neurotypicals often misunderstand neurodivergent ways of communicating just as much as the other way around.

I bring this up as we often pay the price with viewing ourselves negatively due to repeated miscommunications and the blame we place on ourselves (as well as by others). We blame ourselves for not having friends, we blame ourselves for failed relationships, we blame ourselves for feeling lonely, we blame ourselves for being bullied, and we believe that we deserve to feel this miserable because we are the only ones who are labelled as having deficits when it comes to social communication and sustaining relationships.

However, what is often not taken into account before seeing a person as less than is whether the people we have interacted with are being ableist and have not sought to understand those who communicate differently than they do. We may be stuck in a small town, with a limited number of people to socialise with, meaning that there are not people nearby who could be potential friends. There also could be many other reasons as well, but it is important to know we are not failures or less worthy for not communicating neurotypically, despite society trying to tell us otherwise. Many neurodivergent people I have spoken with (including autistic ADHDers) have had difficulties with friendship over the years, but over time they have managed to find the right people to develop friendships with, which has helped with their overall happiness and personal self-acceptance.

I went on a bit of a tangent there (in true neurodivergent style) so coming back to the social model and medical model as concepts, they both come from theories about disability. Now, not everybody will view autism and/or ADHD as disabilities, but they are both formally recognised as disabilities. As individuals, some of us will find our autism and ADHD can be disabling, and consequently consider ourselves to be disabled and may view this as part of our identity, while other autistic ADHDers will not.

Some of us will have a more nuanced view, where we consider ourselves to be disabled but only from a social model perspective. Others will view their neurodivergence as disabling in some ways but that it can also be the reason for some of their strengths. An example could be that you struggle with short-term memory and other executive-functioning-related tasks, but have strong attention to detail. It is also important to point out that some of us will see ourselves as disabled (due to our autism and ADHD) from a more medical viewpoint too, while others may relate to aspects within both the medical and social model of disability that represent their experiences. Again, just because we are autistic ADHDers, it does not mean we all share the same perspective. How disabled we may be by our autism and ADHD will also depend on our personal situation and our ability to access any support we may need, so how privileged we are can also play a role here and influence how we view our autism and ADHD in relation to disability.

For me, I see myself as disabled, as the challenges I experience every day do make it that much harder compared to my neurotypical peers. I also need adjustments to sustain work and to have a fair chance of succeeding in education. I view my disability primarily through the social model, as I feel that if we lived in a different society that wasn't so heavily set up for people who are 'normal', I would face fewer barriers as an autistic ADHDer. Although, no matter how autism and ADHD friendly a society could be, I think I would always struggle with aspects related to executive functioning to some degree. The social model was not a concept I was aware of until I started to engage with neurodivergent people, but it was helpful to my self-acceptance, as it helped me see that a lot of the things I harshly blamed on myself before were not actually my fault. Some examples of things I blamed myself for included struggling with long commutes on top of full time work (while most people managed no problem) and people treating me poorly due to my differences.

The social model is a viewpoint, so it won't magically resolve all our problems overnight (if only!), but it can be a helpful way to better understand some of our experiences as autistic ADHDers in this world, beyond only looking at autism and ADHD as a list of deficits. For myself, this has resulted in being less self-critical about things I cannot manage because of my autism and ADHD, which has been part of my own personal journey towards self-acceptance.

Also just because you are an autistic ADHDer does not mean you have to see yourself as disabled, but for some of us disability will be part of our experience. If we are disabled, then understanding how this affects us and who we are will be part of developing our own identity as we come into adulthood. One of the autistic ADHDers I spoke with when writing this book shared how although there are certain parts of their autism and ADHD that were disabling, this did not necessarily mean they saw themselves as disabled:

> 66 I mean, don't get me wrong. Yes, some parts can be disabling, like, standing next to a loudspeaker and I feel like I'm gonna collapse, or when a siren goes past I have to hold my ears. That's disabling, but then the rest of it is enabling for me. But I also realised that that's not everybody's experience, because everybody experiences it differently.

The word disability itself often comes with a lot of negative connotations and stigma, which can put people off identifying themselves as disabled (even if they know deep down they are disabled and experience ableism). However, being disabled isn't a moral failure or a bad thing, it is a term to say that we have difficulties and challenges that impact on our daily lives (that most other people don't have). To be honest, it is often people who have very little understanding of disability who incorrectly use the word in a stigmatising way. Being disabled can be hard for some people to accept about themselves, but understanding the difference between negative stereotypes/preconceptions about disability and reality can help us with accepting we are disabled (if that is indeed the case).

Also a lot of people assume that disabilities can only be physical, or that we can always tell if somebody is disabled just by looking at them. Again, this is not correct! Both autism and ADHD are often referred to as either 'hidden disabilities' or 'invisible disabilities', meaning we cannot tell if somebody is autistic, an ADHDer or both solely on appearance. Despite this, there are still stereotypes of how neurodivergent people appear to the outside world, mainly due to how the media often portrays us. A prime example is Sheldon Cooper with both his personality and appearance fitting the common stereotype that exists about autistic people (white geeky male), even though most autistic people won't fit this exact stereotype. Some people may feel as if they cannot identify as disabled because they are not in a wheelchair and do not need physical adaptations to help with their movements. However, there is no one way to be disabled, and disability covers a broad range of people and their experiences, including those of us who are neurodivergent. So if you do consider yourself disabled, but won't identify as such due to not fitting the stereotype of disability, then this is me telling you that you can, and being disabled should not be gatekept on this basis.

Not all of us see ourselves as disabled, but I am aware that many autistic ADHDers do. How much being disabled will be part of our identity will vary massively for each of us; for some it may be a significant part of our identity, whereas for others being disabled will only play a small part (if any). It often comes down to our unique experiences when navigating this world and if disability has shaped who we are as we come into adulthood.

Autistic joy and finding our happiness

So far in this chapter we have primarily talked about the difficulties that some autistic ADHDers may experience when trying to understand who we are in this world as we begin our journeys into adult life. Although it is important to be honest about the difficulties many of us have experienced during our late teens and into our early twenties, it would be a lie to say it is all bad. In fact parts can be fun, exciting and joyful! Neurotypical or not, most people during this time will likely have a mix of both positive and negative experiences related to becoming an adult.

However, something that neurotypicals do not experience are the joys we get from specifically being neurodivergent. A recent term that has come from autistic people to describe this is 'autistic joy'. Autistic joy is the happiness we experience that comes from being autistic – and being ADHDers too doesn't mean we are excluded from experiencing it; indeed we can experience joy based on our ADHD experiences as well. Some aspects of being autistic ADHDers can bring positivity into our lives and provide us joy that we wouldn't experience otherwise (at least to the same level), and seeing this starting to be celebrated is wonderful, especially with such a long history of autism and ADHD being seen through a negative lens.

One example of how I found joy from my ADHD was embracing some of my hyperactive responses. I normally hate running, but sometimes I get a sudden burst of energy and I do just run and go with it. It only usually lasts for a couple of seconds, but just being able to move in the way my mind and body wants rejuvenates my energy, clears my mind and brings me joy. How often this happens varies a lot, but when I feel a need to and it's safe to do so (which usually means when I am at home), it is something that brings me happiness.

Joy that comes from being autistic is often related to what has become frequently labelled as 'special interests'. I know there are mixed views on this term specifically, but there is no denying that autistic people's areas of interests do provide us with a source of happiness when engaging in them, researching the topic or doing activities related to our interests. Examples of these might be stereotypical, such as train or plane spotting, or something other people wouldn't expect, such as interest in a boy band or participating in a certain sport. For myself, autistic joy comes from several areas. I experience sensory joy from being in water, which is why swimming is my favourite sport and main form of physical activity, and I experience it when I am playing *The Sims* or watching classic Disney films, or Googling niche facts when I want to find something out I don't know yet (I do this a lot and usually end up down a Wikipedia rabbit hole, sometimes for hours!).

Also one fellow autistic ADHDer shared some of the positive qualities that come from their neurodivergence and the joy these bring them personally:

66 My hyperaware brain makes me extremely observant with a good eye for detail; my hyperfixations on new information and love of categorising facts gives me an intense enthusiasm for learning about EVERYTHING.

As you can see, the joy we can experience from being neuro-divergent will vary for each of us, but everybody I talked with while writing this book had at least one thing that brought them joy from being neurodivergent. Knowing and appreciating our sources of joy is a key part of understanding who we are and getting to a place where we can accept ourselves. Remember that if we were not autistic ADHDers, we would not have the same levels of happiness in our interests, nor would our lives be as enriched by them.

Working towards self-acceptance

When people talk about self-acceptance, what they are usually referring to is being content (or happy) with who we are, including not only the parts of ourselves that we like, but also the parts of ourselves we may see or feel are personal flaws (even if this isn't true!). Most people struggle with self-acceptance on some level, particularly during our early adult years, when there is great pressure to conform to the social norms around us. However, when we throw being autistic ADHDers into the mix, self-acceptance can be even more difficult. Depending on your experiences to date, you may either have positive, negative or mixed feelings about being neurodivergent. In an ideal world, it would be a positive for us if we could all unapologetically be as open with our neurodivergence as we wished, but reality can be very different for many of us still, which can have a knock-on effect on our self-worth and our identity too.

When looking to develop our own self-acceptance, for some (depending on our past experiences) it can seem like an alien concept to start with. I think one of the first steps in a journey towards greater self-acceptance is realising where we are starting from, and the reasons why we may have low self-acceptance. Again, other factors will massively affect our starting points, but it is safe to assume that many autistic ADHDers' self-acceptance will be at a lower starting point because of the discrimination many of us faced throughout our childhood and teen years. Nonetheless, even if we've had a primarily negative self-view of being an autistic ADHDer up until now does not mean this will always be the case. Building a more positive view of ourselves can take time and is often a gradual process. One of the autistic ADHDers I spoke with shared part of their journey towards self-acceptance:

> 66 I suppose quote unquote stereotypical neurodivergence, even now I'm having a hard time accepting that applies to me and like it's okay; it's like I can be, you know, I can be almost 23 and, like, enjoy sleeping with a stuffed animal – that doesn't make me some weird creep, that's fine. But it was just drilled into you, like cringe culture.

So although they recognise that they enjoy sleeping with a stuffed animal and know that there is nothing wrong with doing so, they still can find it difficult to accept they do this, due to societal views of adults sleeping with stuffed animals. It can take a long time to move past unnecessary stigma, and often there will be in-between phases such as 'I know this is okay, but I still feel guilty about doing X, Y or Z'. However, it is possible to get to a point where we can do these things without feeling guilty. It will often take time, and many repetitions of doing things that may be deemed 'cringe' by others before we start to feel more comfortable with doing them. Also, we should not pressure ourselves to feel 100% comfortable with doing things that we have previously faced stigma for, as letting go of the stigma is usually a gradual process. Trying to force automatic acceptance will often pile on additional pressure and may lead to us denying the full emotions we are experiencing when starting to do the stigmatised things again (in essence, we may gaslight ourselves without realising). It is okay to take our time to become comfortable again with doing the things we enjoy and be more self-accepting.

Even though I did not know growing up that I was an autistic ADHDer, I did have a fairly negative view of the aspects of myself that related to both my autism and ADHD. I think this was mainly due to being in a hostile environment at school, as my needs were completely unmet, and I was also vulnerable to abuse from other students; staff either chose to ignore what was going on or did not do anything to stop it. Naturally, most people in these circumstances would not have a positive self-image or view of their identity.

Although I was in a bad place during my school years, the feelings of extreme self-hatred that came from this period thankfully did not last. But my negative self-view did not disappear overnight! Leaving school was the first step out of a toxic environment for me, and the first towards a place where I was able to become more self-accepting (even if I did not know it at the time). I still experience the effects of the trauma from those years, and it took discovering that I was an autistic ADHDer to understand that what I went through wasn't my fault, despite being made to feel that way before. Having the knowledge of what autism and ADHD are, what they mean for me and how they affect my life has enabled me to question the self-blame I had felt for decades. I realise now that I was not to blame, and that I had been hating on my neurodivergent qualities and challenges due to how I had been treated by others, rather than hating who I truly am.

Again this did not happen overnight but gradually as I reflected back on the past situations and realised the reasons why I viewed myself so negatively. One of the biggest parts of being more self-accepting as an autistic ADHDer was realising my self-view was based on other people's bigotry and ignorance in combination with not having the right space growing up to openly explore who I was unmasked and away from these people.

One of the good things about becoming an adult is we will usually have more flexibility in where we spend our time, and who we spend it with. Having more freedom has meant I am now able to find times where I can be alone and do what I enjoy guilt free, while also choosing who to socialise with (and how often). Over time, having this freedom as I have come into my adult years has meant I have been able to get to know myself better away from the toxicity, learn about the things I love about myself, and realise that I don't hate myself for qualities I had previously viewed so negatively. Granted, there are still things that I don't 100% love about myself (very few people have none of these to be honest, even if they never admit it) and I still experience real challenges related to my neurodivergence, but I am in a place now where I am content with who I am as a person, including my flaws, and it is a relief that I do not spend so much time hating myself. It is important to know we are not a problem or less than for being autistic ADHDers, even if others have made us feel that way.

However, when some of us first realise we are different from our peers, or come to realise that we are neurodivergent, we may not want a label like autism or ADHD as we can often experience shame for not being neurotypical or for having autistic and ADHD characteristics. At first, many of us may see the things that make us neurodivergent primarily in a negative light, due to people's comments, responses, treatment of us and judgement of our differences. Again, we do not even need to have the knowledge yet that we are autistic ADHDers to feel this way, as one fellow autistic ADHDer explains – they felt something was wrong with them before discovering they were neurodivergent:

> 66 It felt as if there was always something fundamentally wrong with me... it was almost like I had to do a process of elimination. Like most people who were socialised as girls had issues with my body and I did hate my body to an extent, but that wasn't the whole picture. So I worked through that. And then I was maybe about 17 or 18 pretty okay with my body after years of hating it, and that's okay, but I still felt like there's something wrong with me, that it has nothing to do with my body.

So for some of us, we may be coming from a place where we are trying to identify what is 'wrong' with us as part of our journey towards better understanding ourselves and self-acceptance. Even though now I am more self-accepting, I came from a similar place when trying to figure why I was struggling so much with managing the demands of everyday life. I came to realise that there was something more significant going on than just anxiety and depression, and I assumed automatically that this must be a significantly bad thing. What was actually happening was that as an autistic ADHDer I had gone over 20 years with no support while trying to force myself to function like a neurotypical, with others placing these expectations on me too.

Part of my own self-acceptance journey has been realising that I am not a failure for the struggles I had, and that the parts I originally hated about myself were due to my autism and ADHD, and there was never anything wrong or bad with my way of being. Understanding that the world we live in is not set up for brains like ours has helped to relieve the self-blame I was constantly feeling before.

Self-acceptance can also be realising the limitations we may have from living in a neurotypical world (I know this may seem like a strange thing to say, but it will become clear in the next few paragraphs!). In our society that is so focused on 'normal', it is often implied that normality is the route to all happiness for everyone.

I used to believe this, and as a result, tried to make everything about myself as 'normal' as possible, but it just made me miserable and led to burnout. One example of this is accepting that I cannot socialise as much as everybody expects me to. I have to be okay with some people thinking I'm 'letting them down' as my mind and body need time to recharge the social batteries away from people. As masking was so ingrained into my being when I was younger, this came hand in hand with people pleasing, to the point I was negating my own personal needs. I had to accept that if I was going to take proper care of myself, I needed to respect my own needs before putting myself in situations where they would be compromised. It is not easy, especially when potential rejection from others can be emotionally intense. However, it is important to think about what will be better in the long term. And for me this meant I started to become less of a people pleaser.

Interestingly enough one of the autistic ADHDers I interviewed for this book also opened up about how realising their limits was a big part of their self-acceptance journey, but in a different way to my own:

> It sort of started with realising the life I had thought I wanted, I can no longer have and then learning to accept that. Learning to make peace with the lifestyle I now have and then trying to figure out how I can try to live the best life I can with what I have now but yeah, I guess it was quite a tricky journey.

Accepting limitations can be a hard thing to do, as it can feel like doors are closing to us just because we are not neurotypical or because of the disabling factors we have from autism, ADHD and other co-existing conditions. However, just because some doors may close to us does not mean our lives are over. It often can put us on a new path that we didn't expect to take. Along the way we may have obstacles and setbacks, but sometimes other things will come our way that are better suited to us, and that we wouldn't have encountered otherwise.

If you asked me at 18 what direction I thought I wanted my life to go in, I would never have guessed I would be where I am now. Part of that was accepting I couldn't do certain jobs, or live the lifestyle that was expected of me and that most of the people I grew up around were able to follow. Although it was hard at first to accept this, over several years I was able to learn what does work for me, and what I am able do, and build my life around that. A big part was trial and error, as the answers I needed on what kind of lifestyle I could sustain did not become clear overnight, and it certainly has not been a smooth ride (trust me, it took years!). But it was worth it, as I am much happier than I would have been if I had gone down the more conventional path I wanted when I was younger.

This has been a big part of my self-acceptance too, knowing that I am not a failure for not going down the conventional path that others were expecting (and sometimes pressuring) me to. Accepting that what made me happy was different from most others because of my autism and ADHD, and that it was okay to be that way. For sure many people question my life decisions now and judge them in a negative way, but my happiness is more important than some stranger's opinion trying to guilt trip me into living in a generic neurotypical way that will make me unhappy at best, and have significant consequences for my mental health at worst. I have come to realise that the paths that were closed off to me, making me feel limited, were never going to work out. And ultimately my life has ended up going in a much better direction as a result.

When asking the same autistic ADHDer quoted above more about what happened when they realised their limits, they opened up about how they were still able to do other things that were fulfilling to them, even though it was not what they thought they wanted when they first discovered their autism and ADHD:

66 Like, growing up, I always hated who I was. I knew I was different. I didn't fit in, everything just seemed a lot more difficult. And then I found out I was autistic. Is that me? Figuring it out, it's been really tough because it's almost been like a journey that's taken many, many years. Because before my diagnosis, I had a path to follow that I knew I wanted. I wanted to go and be either an electrician or carpenter, an accountant or an IT technician, right. Those are my options. That was my life path. I'm gonna go down that path. As soon as I was diagnosed with the conditions (including autism and ADHD) it was like, well, that's impossible now. You can't reach there. I think that was the most difficult part because that's what I wanted to do. Then I wanted to be an IT technician. And then that kind of fell through because of my grades a little bit. Yeah, and then I ended up working with adults with learning disabilities for four years. Volunteering for Hearts and Minds (the former peer

support charity) for five years and volunteering with the Dig-
ital Champions for five years. Nowhere near where I thought
I was gonna be. But yeah, I guess that was the thing that was
the most tricky, was having the goal of where I wanted to be
and then it was just removed, and sort of okay, well, this is
what I got now.

Just because we are autistic ADHDers does not mean our lives
are over, or that everything will be miserable. We may face
challenges with being neurodivergent in a neurotypical world,
but that does not mean that there is nothing out there for us.
For many of us, having a purpose we can fulfil and being able
to engage with the things we enjoy are often key parts of our
self-acceptance journey as autistic ADHDers. If you have not
found your purpose yet, it may be worth starting with the interests you have and see what is out there or what you can get
involved with that is related. Some of us do them purely because
of the joy they bring to our lives, while for others they may lead
us into jobs and careers. The most important thing is that you
are doing these things for yourself and nobody else, as part of
self-acceptance is doing what makes us happy, regardless of what
other people think.

Another common narrative that we may come across in our journey towards self-acceptance is that 'autism is a super power', and
articles online that read 'Here are 20 super successful people
with ADHD'. Although this may make some autistic ADHDers
feel positive about themselves initially, it can have an unintended
negative impact on others, as we can end up feeling like we can
only be accepted by society as neurodivergent if we are the
next Albert Einstein. One of the autistic ADHDers I spoke with

experienced a lot of pressure to excel in certain areas of their life due to being an autistic ADHDer and feeling the need to compensate for their differences:

> 66 Okay, but if I have to be autistic, then I'll make sure that I'm one of those ones that's like really smart. And I pressured myself to do really well. I mean, I did pretty well at school anyway, but then I would like put extra pressure on myself. I feel like I had to prove myself more and that I had to kind of balance out this bad thing by doing better in other areas... Like I don't agree with any of it now, but it will be almost thoughts along the lines of 'I won't make it an inconvenience for everyone else'.

It is important for us to recognise our strengths when discovering and accepting who we are (we will talk more about this in a little bit), but it can come at a cost if we feel the pressure to 'prove' our strengths to people who underestimate us or view us negatively because we are neurodivergent. It is important to recognise our own strengths and qualities, but we should not be put in a position where people will only respect autistic ADHDers if they value our talents or perceived strengths, and not the whole authentic version of ourselves. These people are not true friends and may seek to take advantage of us, so please do be mindful of anyone you feel you need to prove yourself to in order to gain respect.

Another effect of 'autism and ADHD are my super powers' is that we may start to see ourselves as better than other autistic ADHDers who have different support needs and abilities from us, because we can be successful in some areas that not all autistic ADHDers are (even if it comes at a huge emotional cost). We can find ways to accept and celebrate ourselves, positive qualities and strengths that do not put down our fellow neurodivergent people.

Self-acceptance can feel like a tricky thing to navigate as autistic ADHDers. I do see things starting to change, with autistic ADHDers sharing their experiences online (rather than having their voices drowned out by neurotypicals constantly), including celebrating who they are and their differences, which was rarely the case before. Although there is still a long way to go for wider acceptance, it is encouraging to see a shift towards autistic ADHDers sharing the positive aspects of their lives and identities, and no longer seeing being neurodivergent as the end of the world! It is great and refreshing to see others being able to express the joys they experience from being neurodivergent, which they likely had to hide before. And for some of us, seeing this representation (that really didn't exist even a few years ago) can be a real positive in helping us to become more accepting of who we are.

It is wonderful to see neurodivergent people, including autistic ADHDers, provide a more positive representation of our experiences online and in the media. However, one unintended impact of online content like this can be some autistic ADHDers feeling pressure to only view their autism and ADHD as being a totally positive aspect of their lives 100% of the time. Although that may be the case for some people, for most of us autistic ADHDers our daily lives are different from social media and we all have our good days and bad days. We may also have times in our lives where we view our neurodivergence as a negative, and other times where we view it more positively. One autistic ADHDer opened up honestly about the reasons why they were still not self-accepting at the time I spoke with them:

66 Acceptance as an autistic ADHDer? No – and that is contributed by low self-esteem and poor mental health.

Thinking back to my school days, it would be impossible to expect anybody who was in my previous situation to see their neurodivergence as only a positive aspect of themselves at that time. Reading positive social media posts about being autistic ADHDers would likely not have made a difference. So even though I am more self-accepting now of my neurodivergent self, there were times where even the smallest amount of self-acceptance would have been impossible due to my personal situation.

Across our lives, we will likely have a mix of experiences which impact our self-view and how much we are self-accepting of being autistic ADHDers. It is okay if we are going through a more difficult time, and we are struggling with accepting our authentic selves. Chances are that the last thing we need is additional pressure to force self-acceptance on ourselves when times are hard! There will be times where being self-accepting as autistic ADHDers will be easier than others. Life is rarely a straight line going upwards towards happiness, so it is okay if our own individual paths to self-acceptance go up and down too.

Other people's views when working towards self-acceptance

As we start to actively practise self-acceptance, others may notice changes in how we present to the outside world. Responses from others can vary massively, and depending on our personal circumstances we may want to pick carefully when and where we either unmask, open up about our neurodivergence or both. If we find a space that feels safe enough or right for us to open up to those around us about our autism and/or ADHD, hopefully it will go well, which is often a huge relief and can be a confidence boost. However, we may also come across people who are less understanding and more judgemental or dismissive. A common response from people who make these assumptions is that we are making everything up. Hearing comments like this can be very difficult, especially if we are working towards self-acceptance and are becoming more open about our autism and ADHD with others as part of our journey. Although some people will be understanding, unfortunately not everybody will be.

The challenge is figuring out who is safe for us to be open with, which can be harder than we think. Personally, I have found it really hit and miss when opening up with other people, including some people I was close with not being understanding (or even trying to understand). Sometimes it may be a case of trial and error, or seeking out other neurodivergent and/or understanding people who are willing to listen. It may not necessarily be those we are closest with who are the best people to talk to about developing our self-acceptance of being autistic ADHDers. That is something I unfortunately learnt the hard way, as not everyone was as supportive as I assumed they would be. If we are knocked back when opening up about our differences around people who we thought were safe, it can impact our confidence to open up again.

It is okay if you need to take your time to process a negative response before considering opening up to others about being neurodivergent again. The most important thing is that we are compassionate to ourselves when these situations happen. They are not our fault, and often any negative response we receive says a lot more about the other person than us. Just because we may not have yet found the people who we can open up to about being autistic ADHDers does not mean they are not out there – we have just not found them yet. Once we feel ready, we can try again to find people who we can comfortably open up to, or they may come into our lives when we least expect it.

Something else I have learnt from starting to be more open about my neurodivergence in recent years is that is has become a test of who in my life is prepared to accept me unconditionally as my authentic self, and who is not. Although it has been painful to discover somebody was not as accepting as I thought they would be when I started to mask less or opened up, it showed me who I could trust, and who was not worth continuing any form of friendship/relationship with. Part of my own self-acceptance is no longer appeasing people who cannot appreciate the real me and knowing that I do not have to compromise myself anymore for people who are ableist towards my neurodivergence. I do not have to keep anyone in my life who is making me feel worse for being different. It is okay, and sometimes necessary, to let people go, drift away or cut off contact in order to further develop our own self-acceptance. It can be hard to do in the moment, but your own peace is priceless, especially if someone's attitude towards you is a barrier to being happy with who you are.

Another challenge we may face when trying to become more accepting of ourselves is lack of understanding or the opinions of neurodivergence from family, or other people we may be forced to interact with when growing up. If these have been negative, including poor responses to our differences, we may have lower self-esteem or even trauma. An all too common experience of this that many of us have been subjected to is being compared to children, with the implicit question being 'Why aren't you more like your friend/sibling/cousin or the neighbour's child?'

Obviously the exact wording of this comment can vary, but it can be crushing to our self-acceptance when people compare us to neurotypicals with the desire for us to 'be like them'. It is also comments like this that can pressure us into masking. Often this message may not have been communicated directly, but implied in different ways. An example of this is when we are told to do certain things or socialise like other neurotypicals our age, or growing up we notice that other children are being praised for things that are neurotypical in nature, while our teachers and parents fail to discover and recognise our strengths or only point out our differences in a negative light.

If we have experienced this (or similar examples) and it has had a knock-on effect with our self-esteem and acceptance, it can feel really hard to move forwards. Especially if these comments came from people close to us, or who we trusted when we were younger. If it has had a particularly significant impact on us, then we may want to seek support from others to work through the difficulties we face because of our past experiences. However, that isn't our only option. We can also decide to discover our own strengths and positive qualities. It can be hard to know where to start with this, but we can try the following:

- Think about what you enjoy doing and the joy that comes from doing these things.
- What have we done that resulted in a positive outcome? Or changed something for the better?
- Ask others we trust or who know us well what they see as our strengths and positive qualities.

Ultimately, we do not have to continue believing any false narrative or lack of recognition about our qualities. Part of becoming more accepting of ourselves is recognising the false and negative comments that have been made about us growing up, and starting to see the good aspects of ourselves, doing the things that give us joy, and knowing what our talents are.

Now we have looked at various factors autistic ADHDers may face when working towards their own self-acceptance, I thought I would end this chapter by sharing the most positive aspects of my own self-acceptance journey – which is still ongoing, but I am certainly in a better place now than I was several years ago! Your journey may differ from mine, as all our journeys to self-acceptance will be unique, but there may be some similarities or overlap since we are autistic ADHDers.

For most people there will be things we like about who we are, and parts we are not so keen on. Self-acceptance often includes recognising that we are not perfect beings, but we can still be happy with who we are. I accept that skills relating to my executive functioning make my life more difficult, and that comes from my neurodivergence. But at the same time if I wasn't neurodivergent, I would also be missing out on a lot of the joy I experience from my interests, and not have such a positive connection with my cat, who is my absolute fur baby and is a big part of my world. So although there are negative aspects to being neurodivergent for myself, I accept that if I was suddenly to become neurotypical overnight, there would be a lot of good things in my life that would go away too, things that I would never want to give up. Part of my own self-acceptance has been realising that being 'perfect' would mean compromising on things that give me happiness and joy, which I am not willing to do. I can still have acceptance of who I am without being 'perfect' or 'normal'.

Letting go of the idea of being 'normal' has been helpful in becoming more accepting of myself as a neurodivergent person. This can be hard when most of us have experienced a lifetime of people trying to make us act 'normal' through masking. To say I am completely unmasked as an autistic ADHDer and I am 100% my authentic self the whole time would be a lie. But accepting that 'normal' will never make me happy, and my happiness exists outside of what the world tells us is 'normal', gives me great relief. It means putting my needs first, rather than everyone else's, and looking after myself rather than holding myself to a standard that never added value to my life anyway.

It would have been impossible to become more self-accepting without realising that obsessing over being 'normal' all the time was reducing my quality of life a lot. At the same time, I don't think I could have come to realise this without discovering I was an autistic ADHDer –having this knowledge and understanding of my neurodivergence has been a vital part of my own self-acceptance.

Becoming more self-accepting has also meant realising I cared too much about other people's opinions of my neurodivergent differences. Naturally this came from a need to mask my autism and ADHD for many years, which meant I didn't do the things that made me happy. Making the time now to do the things I love and enjoy rather than feeling pressured to socialise in a neurotypical way has helped self-acceptance to come more easily. Over time I am increasingly devaluing the opinions of people who don't even care about me yet will still judge. It is not an easy thing to do, and can't be done overnight, but starting to care a little less daily about people who are not important to me has really helped with my happiness.

Growing up, I thought self-acceptance meant changing yourself to the point where everything was ideal, and that people could only be accepting of themselves if they did not have any flaws. Coming into adulthood made me realise that this was literally impossible for anyone, regardless of their neurotype. Understanding that everybody has their good days and not so good days meant it was easier to be accepting of who I am without being perfect. Having this acceptance, along with the other changes I made in my life to be more accommodating to my neurodivergent needs, has meant there are more good days now than before, even if not everything is perfect, and that is totally okay.

7
Conclusion

My discovery that I was autistic – and not long after that I was an ADHDer – came at a point when I was struggling to navigate my early adult years. Everything from the relationships I had to trying to secure a job (and a fair amount of bouncing from one job to another) made me realise that there was something more significant going on than experiencing a few specific challenges, which eventually led to discovering the full extent of my neurodivergence.

The motivation for writing this book was that a lot of the struggles I had were either avoidable or worsened by the fact I didn't know I was an autistic ADHDer, and I was clueless about things that could have helped make day-to-day life easier. Through engaging with many neurodivergent people I saw that I was not the only person to have these struggles when coming into adulthood (I genuinely thought that I was the only one before) and that many of us have similar stories of why things have been more difficult for us compared to our friends and siblings during this period of our lives.

As autistic ADHDers reading this book, I hope that you have been able to take something useful away from it, and from some of the experiences that other autistic ADHDers have gone through before and shared here, so that you do not have to struggle as much as others have previously as young adults. For some, simply having knowledge of what autism and ADHD are can be the starting point – especially if we did not find out we are autistic ADHDers until later on in life. That is why this book starts by introducing autism and ADHD, as some of us are likely still trying to understand why so many things in our past either didn't make sense or go as we planned. Starting to gain this awareness can be a significant turning point in our life and help us to put the dots together of how many of our experiences have been related to autism and ADHD.

A common source of the challenges autistic ADHDers experience is executive functioning and how our short-term memory, task switching, impulsivity, sequencing and time blindness have an impact on our lives, whether we are at home, in university or college or while working. Although executive functioning is something that would have affected us while at school, it affects us more as we take on more responsibilities in adulthood. Also, if we have been using certain strategies to cope, they may not be as effective as we move into different environments, e.g. going from school to university, so we may need to adapt them to help us thrive in our new situation. Hopefully the ideas and suggestions in this book on executive functioning can be a starting point for finding out what works best for you as an individual.

When we transition into adulthood, we are often faced with a lot of new situations, which can feel incredibly overwhelming as autistic ADHDers. In the book we went through some of the differences that come along with being an adult, which will hopefully demystify what you can expect – something that is not always talked about openly or in a way which is clear for autistic ADHDers to understand. In this period we also must make decisions that will often affect our lives in a significant way, which can be exciting but also stressful. Not knowing where to even start when it comes to making big life choices for the first time can feel like a major hurdle. The experiences of the autistic ADHDers who contributed to this book can give some insight into how others have approached decision making, and this was accompanied by some guidance to help you think about how you might like to make decisions for yourself.

As relationships and socialising are often a significant part of our lives, it was important to consider how our interactions are different during our early adult years, including new types of relationships that we may not have had before. For many autistic ADHDers, we have likely had a lot of mixed experiences with relationships growing up and our social interactions can feel like a minefield! To try to make the social minefield less confusing, both fellow autistic ADHDers and myself have opened up about the different types of relationships we've experienced and how we navigated them, along with managing how much we socialise. For most of us it really has been a case of trial and error over the years, so opening up about our social experiences will hopefully make things easier for you than it was for us.

Another important aspect of our lives is emotional well-being and mental health. As autistic ADHDers we often have differ-ence in how we express our emotions and experience our mental health. Acknowledging these differences, and what is important for autistic ADHDers' well-being, is vital for us to be properly supported (if needed) and to prevent things getting worse. Also, we may have experienced difficulties related to our mental health and well-being when we were younger, but with the challenges and additional pressures that come along with reaching adult-hood, we may become more vulnerable to having difficulties in this area. The insight shared by fellow autistic ADHDers will hopefully provide some comfort in knowing that you are not the only person going through these experiences or struggles. And also help you to recognise you may not have been given the best advice, treatment or therapies before because your neurodiver-gence was not taken into account. That in itself can be lifesaving, as it can help prevent further harm by avoiding places or people that were never fully capable of supporting us.

As we become young adults, it is a significant time for us to discover who we are and learn about what we enjoy and want to do with our lives (along with the things we will certainly not like too!). Often as autistic ADHDers there will be additional things we need to consider when coming to understand who we are as adults and accepting ourselves. Although this is not easy and often happens over a long period of time, the different journeys shared by autistic ADHDers in this book will hopefully provide some insight into how people were able to become more self-accepting and better understand themselves. Our journeys towards knowing who we are and self-acceptance will always be unique to some degree, but having the awareness of how autism and ADHD can affect our understanding of who we are will make it that little bit easier to be content with our own identity.

We have covered a lot in this book on different ways we can make life easier to navigate as we come into adulthood as autistic ADHDers, and I hope that the content of the book has been a stepping stone to help you figure out some of the new challenges and opportunities that come along with being an adult. However, it is important to remember that it is not all on us. The lack of understanding in our society about neurodivergent people can create further challenges (which are often avoidable) for autistic ADHDers. So please do not feel like you are a failure if the suggestions here do not resolve everything that is going on in your lives. Wider societal changes are needed so that all autistic ADHDers can thrive, which is not our individual responsibility, but we can still come together to advocate for these wider changes.

Although growing up as autistic ADHDers isn't always easy, it does not mean that we won't find happiness and joy in our lives. These things are just as possible for us as anybody else, but we will likely need to travel less conventional paths to understand who we are and to live a life we are truly content with as autistic ADHDers.

Glossary

Ableism – Discrimination based on disability or being neurodivergent.

Alexithymia – Difficulties with describing your own emotions.

AuDHDer – Another term for autistic ADHDer.

Autistic ADHDer – Somebody who is both autistic and an ADHDer.

Executive function – How our brains process information and work to complete tasks often related to organising and planning.

Masking/camouflaging – Having to act like a neurotypical person in social situations for your own safety and/or to gain acceptance from others.

Monotropism – A natural tendency to focus on a smaller number of interests (making it difficult to focus on everything in the environment at once).

Multiply-neurodivergent – A person whose brain works differently than most other people's in more than one way. E.g. autism and ADHD.

Neurodivergence – How your thinking differs from normal/neurotypical people.

Neurodivergent – A person whose brain works differently from the norm.

Neurodiversity – The natural diversity of human brains.

Neurotypical – A person whose brain works in a similar way to most other people.

Time blindness – Struggling with having a sense of time when it comes to completing tasks and activities.

Bibliography

Autistic Inertia. (2022). *Home: Autistic Inertia*. Retrieved from Autistic Inertia: http://autisticinertia.com/

Beardon, L. (2020). *Avoiding Anxiety in Autistic Children*. Sheldon Press.

Boon, S. (2020). *Did my ADHD mask my autism? (and vice-versa)*. Retrieved from Autistically Sarah: http://autisticallysarah.com/2020/09/25/did-my-adhd-mask-my-autism-and-vice-versa/

Botha, M., Chapman, R., Giwa Onaiwu, M., Kapp, S. K., Stannard Ashley, A., & Walker, N. (2024). 'The neurodiversity concept was developed collectively: An overdue correction on the origins of neurodiversity theory'. *Autism*, 0(0). https://doi.org/10.1177/13623613241237871

Curnow E., Utley I., Rutherford M., Johnston L., & Maciver D. (2023). *Diagnostic assessment of autism in adults - current considerations in neurodevelopmentally informed professional learning with reference to ADOS-2. Front Psychiatry*. Retrieved from https://www.ncbi.nlm.nih.gov/pmc/articles/PMC10585137/

Ellzey, L. (2020). *Autism and meltdowns: One autistic woman's journey*. Retrieved from Neuroclastic: https://neuroclastic.com/autism-and-meltdowns-one-autistic-womans-journey/

Fulton, R., Reardon, E., Richardson, K., & Jones, R. (2020). *Sensory trauma: Autism, sensory difference and the daily experience of fear*. Autism Wellbeing.

Gathercole, S. E., Pickering, S. J., Knight, C., & Stegmann, Z. (2004). Working memory skills and educational attainment: Evidence from national curriculum assessments at 7 and 14 years of age. *Applied Cognitive Psychology, 18*(1), 1–16.

How to ADHD. (2019). *How to (actually) get out the door on time*. Retrieved from YouTube: www.youtube.com/watch?v=rC3tG3lbrNM&t=205s

How to ADHD. (2021). *What if I can't tell what I'm feeling? (Alexithymia)*. Retrieved from YouTube: www.youtube.com/watch?v=gyMOSsg3Nps

How to ADHD. (2021). *How to Deal with Rejection Sensitivity*. Retrieved from https://www.youtube.com/watch?v=jM3azhiOy5E

Levy, F. (1991). The dopamine theory of attention deficit hyperactivity disorder (ADHD). *Australian & New Zealand Journal of Psychiatry, 25*(2), 277–283. doi:10.3109/00048679109077746

Mandell, D., Wiggins, L., Carpenter, L., Daniels, J., DiGuiseppi, C., Durkin, M., ... & Kirby, R. (2009). Racial/ethnic disparities in the identification of children with autism spectrum disorders. *American Journal of Public Health, 99*(3), 493–498.

McCrossin, R. (2022). Finding the true number of females with autistic spectrum disorder by estimating the biases in initial recognition and clinical diagnosis. *Children, 9,* 272.

McKay, M. (2020). *The Energy Accounting Activity for Autism.* Retrieved from https://medium.com/age-of-awareness/the-energy-accounting-activity-for-autism-3a245e34bdfb

Milton, D. E. (2012). On the ontological status of autism: The 'double empathy problem'. *Disability & Society, 27*(6), 883–887.

Mind. (2023). *Autism and mental health.* Retrieved from Mind: www.mind.org.uk/about-us/our-policy-work/equality-and-human-rights/autism-and-mental-health/

Miserandino, C. (2003). *The spoon theory.* Retrieved from But You Don't Look Sick: https://butyoudontlooksick.com/articles/written-by-christine/the-spoon-theory/

Murray, F. (2022). *Welcome to Monotropism.org.* Retrieved from Monotropism: https://monotropism.org/

Oliver, M. (2013). 'The social model of disability: thirty years on', *Disability & Society,* 28:7, 1024-1026. Retrieved from https://web.archive.org/web/20160211171559id_/http://www.tandfonline.com/doi/pdf/10.1080/09687599.2013.818773

Walker, N. (n.d.). *Neuroqueer: The Writings of Dr. Nick Walker.* Retrieved from https://neuroqueer.com/neurodiversity-terms-and-definitions

Young Minds. (2023). *A guide for young people; ADHD and mental*

health. Retrieved from Young Minds: www.youngminds.org.uk/
young-person/mental-health-conditions/adhd-and-mental-
health/#ADHDandyourmentalhealth